LAKE COMO TRAVEL GUIDE 2024 Edition:

Your Ultimate Travel Companion To Experiencing the Magic of Italy's Famed Lake Como Through Expert Tips.

SCOTT JOHNSON

TABLE OF CONTENT

Chapter 1: Introduction

Welcome to Lake Como

Welcome to the timeless attraction of Lake Como, where every moment resonates with the beautiful combination of natural magnificence and Italian elegance. As you begin on your voyage through the "Lake Como Travel Guide 2024," visualize a tapestry of turquoise seas, beautiful mountains, and small towns that together build a masterpiece painted by nature itself.

A Symphony of Sights and Sounds:
Picture yourself upon the dazzling beaches of Lake Como, where the beautiful waters reflect the surrounding high peaks. Each village bordering

the lake's side is a chapter in a novel etched in cobblestone alleys, old mansions, and lovely cafés.

Your Passport to Paradise:
This book is more than a compilation of suggestions; it's your passport to the enchanting world of Lake Como. Whether you're a traveler seeking hidden jewels, a connoisseur of culture, or a seeker of calm, Lake Como provides a mosaic of experiences waiting to be explored.

Beyond the Ordinary:
Peel back the layers of traditional travel as we bring you through the essence of Lake Como - from the quaint appeal of Varenna to the magnificence of Bellagio, each moment is an invitation to dive into a world where time appears to slow down.

Why Lake Como:
It's not simply a destination; it's an enchantment. Lake Como calls with its timeless beauty, where every dawn and sunset paints the sky in colours that stay in your mind. It's a spot where the whispers of history meet the current elegance of Italian living.

Your Personal Odyssey:
So, let this book be your friend, your storyteller, and your confidant as you travel the cobblestone alleys and secret nooks of Lake Como. As you flip each page, picture yourself drifting on a boat over the reflecting waters, absorbing the wonder that only Lake Como can generate.

Welcome to a voyage where every scenery is a postcard, every meal a celebration, and every moment an eternal memory. This is Lake Como - a location that transcends the ordinary and encourages you to experience the exceptional. The adventure awaits.

Brief Overview of the Region

Nestled among the magnificent surroundings of Lombardy in Northern Italy, Lake Como emerges as a refuge of natural grandeur and cultural richness. As you begin on a voyage along its beaches, expect to be charmed by the stunning scenery, quaint communities, and a history that threads itself into the fabric of the area.

Geographical Marvel:
Spanning around 146 square kilometers, Lake Como draws attention as the third-largest lake in Italy. Its clean waters cut a Y-shaped masterpiece against the background of the pre-Alpine mountains, producing an ever-changing vista of grandeur that has tempted tourists for millennia.

Township Treasures:
The shores of Lake Como are ornamented with a variety of cities and villages, each a distinct jewel ready to be discovered. From the cobblestone alleyways of Bellagio, where elegance meets simplicity, to the ancient beauty of Como town, the area offers a kaleidoscope of experiences. Varenna, Menaggio, and Tremezzo add to this symphony of variety, guaranteeing there's something for every discriminating tourist.

Echoes of History:
Venture into the past as you explore the lake's edge. Historic homes such as Villa del Balbianello and Villa Carlotta serve as testaments to the region's rich legacy, showing architectural luxury against the gorgeous setting. The air is filled with the whispers of millennia, tempting you to travel back in time.

Cultural Charisma:
Lake Como isn't only a visual feast; it's a cultural adventure. Local festivals, art exhibits, and traditional events inject life into the area, enabling visitors to immerse themselves in the vivid tapestry of Como's cultural character. Here, every cobblestone tells a tale, and every ritual is a celebration.

Elegance and Celebrity Allure:
The beaches of Lake Como have long been a hideaway for the rich, lending a touch of elegance to the area. Historic homes have welcomed luminaries and celebrities, with George Clooney's Villa Oleandra in Laglio standing as an icon of the lake's attractiveness.

Recreation for the Soul:
Beyond its cultural and historical richness, Lake Como draws outdoor lovers. Sail on its blue seas, tour gorgeous hiking paths, or start on leisurely drives around its coastlines. The lake is not simply a destination; it's a recreational paradise, encouraging you to relax and explore.

In this complete review, Lake Como shows itself as more than a destination; it's an experience, an immersion into a world where nature and culture dance in unison, producing a symphony that echoes through the centuries. Welcome to Lake Como, where every moment is a beauty waiting to be found.

What to Expect from the Guide

As you hold this book in your hands, consider it as your own key to uncovering the mysteries and riches of Lake Como. This is more than a simple collection of knowledge; it's a crafted invitation to an engaging and remarkable encounter. Here's what awaits you inside the pages of the "Lake Como Travel Guide 2024":

1. Unveiling Hidden Gems:
Delve into the depths of Lake Como's enchantment as we discover hidden jewels and lesser-known beauties. Beyond the well-trodden pathways, explore quiet nooks, tucked-away cafes, and quaint corners that represent the genuine character of the area.

2. Insider Tips and Local Wisdom:
Navigate Lake Como like a seasoned visitor with our exclusive recommendations. From the optimum times to photograph the dawn over the lake to the secret locations affording panoramic panoramas, we share the local expertise that turns your visit into a genuine and fulfilling trip.

3. Tailored Experiences for Every Traveler:
Whether you're a cultural aficionado, a nature enthusiast, or someone seeking the peacefulness of lakeside getaways, this guide is intended to suit to your individual interests. Find itineraries tailored for various preferences, ensuring that every day unfolds as a customised experience.

4. Culinary Adventures:
Embark on a culinary adventure through the tastes of Lake Como. From rustic trattorias offering traditional regional specialties to elegant lakeside dining, we introduce you to gastronomic pleasures that will excite your taste buds and leave you demanding more.

5. Cultural Immersion:
Immerse yourself in the rich tapestry of Lake Como's culture. Explore local markets, attend traditional festivities, and interact with the warmth of the community. This book acts as your cultural compass, enabling you to engage in the true rhythm of life along the beaches of the lake.

6. Practical Planning Made Effortless:
We understand the value of flawless travel planning. Find extensive information on lodgings, transportation alternatives, and practical

suggestions to guarantee your vacation is not only memorable but also stress-free.

7. Photographic Inspiration:
Capture the majesty of Lake Como via the lens with our photography guide. Discover the most picturesque sites, excellent perspectives, and settings that can lift your vacation photography to new heights. Let the lake become your canvas, and your camera the narrative.

8. Beyond the Guide:
As you visit Lake Como, we invite you to go beyond the tour. Use it as a starting point for accidental discoveries, spontaneous experiences, and intimate interactions that characterise the essence of travel. Lake Como is not simply a destination; it's an open invitation to construct your own tale.

Get ready to open each page and immerse yourself in a world where every word is a stepping stone to a new discovery, and every suggestion is a chance to construct your own Lake Como tale. The trip starts here.

Chapter 2: Getting Started

Planning Your Trip

Embarking on a visit to Lake Como is not just about traveling; it's about arranging a symphony of experiences that connect with your aspirations. In this part, we present you with a path to create your ideal trip to this Italian paradise.

1. Seasonal Symphony:

Unraveling the Seasons: Understand the intricacies of each season surrounding Lake Como, from the bright bloom of spring to the warm charm of winter. Tailor your vacation to match with the mood that resonates best with your travel ambitions.

Festivals & Events: Delve into the cultural calendar of Lake Como. Discover local festivals, art exhibits, and events that might lend an additional layer of enchantment to your stay. This guide assures you don't miss the lifeblood of the area.

2. Crafting Your Itinerary:

Town Tales: Explore the particular charm of each village bordering the coastline. Whether it's the romantic appeal of Bellagio, the historical beauty of Como, or the calm of Varenna, personalize your schedule to fit your interests and pace.

Hidden Gems: Venture off the beaten path with our selected collection of hidden treasures. Secluded locations, lesser-known perspectives, and tucked-away gems await anyone prepared to explore beyond the apparent.

3. Travel Essentials:

Visa and Documentation: Navigate the logistics with ease. Gain insights into visa procedures and ensure you have the essential papers for a smooth arrival into Lake Como.

Transportation Tips: Choose your method of travel intelligently using our transportation guide. Whether you choose for scenic drives, boat journeys, or a mix of both, we present advice to make your travel around the lake as smooth as the water it reflects.

4. Accommodation Alchemy:

Luxury Villas to Cozy Retreats: Discover a diversity of lodgings suited to diverse preferences and budgets. From magnificent lakeside villas to quaint boutique accommodations, we introduce you to alternatives that guarantee your evenings are as wonderful as your days.

Booking Strategies: Learn the art of smart booking to acquire the finest views, positions, and discounts. Our recommendations help you to make educated choices that correspond with your interests.

5. Culinary Chronicles:

Dining Decadence: Delight your palette with our cuisine guide. From classic trattorias to gourmet experiences, we select a list of eating venues that represent the different tastes of Lake Como.

Lakefront Feasts: Experience the enchantment of lakefront dining. Our selections guarantee you relish not only the cuisine but also the environment that makes each meal a memorable affair.

6. Curating Your Own Adventure:

Personalizing Your Journey: This course isn't simply about following a defined route; it's about enabling you to build your own story. Use our choices as a canvas and add your strokes of spontaneity to make your vacation completely unique.

Beyond the Guide: Seize the chance to investigate beyond the suggestions. Whether it's stumbling into a quaint artisan store or engaging in an unplanned chat with locals, Lake Como welcomes you to be an active player in your travel tale.

Prepare to flip the page to a chapter where preparing becomes part of the experience. Your trip to Lake Como awaits, and with this book, every detail is a chance for exploration.

Best Time to Visit

Lake Como, with its ever-changing splendor, provides a special tune for each season. When planning a trip, picking the correct moment is like playing the first note of a symphony. Here we will take you on a journey through the seasons, each of which brings its own enchanting beat to the beaches of Lake Como.

1. Spring Awakening:

Blooms and Beginnings: Lake Como becomes a floral masterpiece when spring arrives. As the hillsides burst into a kaleidoscope of colour, the aroma of wisteria and magnolia fills the air. This is the time of year for rejuvenation, when couples may enjoy peaceful walks through flower gardens and romantic retreats.

Passive Audiences: The spring season is just right, with mild temperatures and fewer people than the summer. Escape the crowds and enjoy the peacefulness of lakeside villages and museums off-season.

2. Summer Serenity:

Azure Waters and Sunny Days: The summer sun sheds its golden light across Lake Como, enticing you to bask in its warmth. Boating trips, lakeside picnics, and al fresco eating become iconic summer events.

Festivals & Events: Summer delivers a variety of activities and festivals. From open-air concerts to lakeside events, immerse yourself in the cultural energy of the area.

Peak Season Energy: Be prepared for a livelier environment as summer brings more guests. Plan your trip intelligently to make the most of major places while also uncovering hidden treasures.

3. Autumn's Palette:

Falling Leaves and Tranquility: As the weather lower and people leave, autumn paints the countryside with warm colors. The reflection of changing foliage on the lake makes a beautiful image.

Wine Harvest and Culinary Delights: Autumn is connected with the grape harvest, making it a great season for wine connoisseurs. Indulge in the scents of the season as local markets exhibit seasonal vegetables and culinary pleasures.

Quiet Elegance: Experience the tranquil side of Lake Como as communities relax into a softer pace. Autumn is a lyrical pause, enabling you to taste the goal at a more leisurely pace.

4. Winter Whispers:

Snow-Capped Peaks and Cozy Evenings: Lake Como takes on a new appeal in winter. Snow-dusted mountains form a magnificent background, while holiday lights cover the cities, providing a touch of enchantment.

Tranquil Retreats: Winter provides an intimate hideaway, great for people seeking quiet. Enjoy lakeside walks, quiet nights by the fireplace, and the attraction of a more intimate atmosphere.

Seasonal Elegance: While certain attractions may have modified hours, winter uncovers a calmer elegance, enabling you to enjoy the region's beauty in a more introspective way.

Choosing Your Crescendo:

Your vacation to Lake Como is not simply a trip; it's a symphony of experiences arranged by the changing seasons. Whether you prefer the flamboyant crescendo of summer or the quiet symphony of winter, each moment is an invitation to immerse yourself in the everlasting appeal of Lake Como. Tailor your vacation to the rhythm that resonates with your spirit, and let the adventure develop in accordance with the seasons.

Visa and Travel Requirements

Embarking on a visit to Lake Como is a foray into a world of magic, and comprehending the visa and travel procedures is the opening to this epic symphony. In this complete guide, we help you through the logistics, ensuring your route to Lake Como is as flawless as the reflections on its tranquil waters.

1. Visa Essentials:

Understanding Schengen: Lake Como sits in the Schengen Area, entailing a uniform visa procedure for 26 European nations. If you are a citizen of a non-Schengen nation, you'll likely require a Schengen Visa to visit Lake Como and its nearby areas.

Visa Categories: Identify the right visa category depending on the objective of your travel - whether it be tourism, business, or other special reasons. Each category comes with its own set of criteria.

2. Pre-Application Preparations:

Passport Validity: Ensure your passport is valid for at least three months after your scheduled departure from the Schengen Area. Check for any extra criteria relevant to your country of origin.

Travel Insurance: Consider purchasing travel insurance that covers health crises and unforeseen incidents. While not essential, it's a prudent precaution for your peace of mind.

Proof of Accommodation and Itinerary: As part of the visa application, you may need to give documentation of your hotel arrangements and a comprehensive itinerary. This is where the preceding parts of your trip guide may be important in planning and documentation.

3. Visa Application Process:

Embassy or Consulate: Locate the closest embassy or consulate of the Schengen nation via which you wish to enter. Visa applications are normally handled by the embassy or consulate of the country you plan to visit first.

Application Forms and Supporting Documents: Familiarize yourself with the relevant paperwork and obtain the essential supporting papers, including evidence of financial resources, round-trip ticket bookings, and travel insurance.

4. Travel Logistics:

Booking Flights: Once your visa is accepted, schedule your tickets to Milan, which serves as a key gateway to Lake Como. Milan Malpensa Airport (MXP) is the major international airport in the area.

Transportation to Lake Como: Plan your continuing route to Lake Como from Milan. Options include rail travel, private transportation, or rental automobiles. Each mode gives a stunning introduction to the area.

5. Additional Travel Tips:

Currency and Payments: Familiarize yourself with the local currency (Euro) and ensure you have adequate cash on hand. Most places also take credit cards.

Language Basics: While English is commonly understood, learning a few basic Italian words may enrich your trip and develop ties with locals.

Ensuring a Harmonious Entry:
Embarking on a Lake Como journey is a voyage into an exquisite world, and comprehending the subtleties of visa and travel procedures is the compass guiding you through the gateway. As you prepare to explore the beaches of

Lake Como, may your voyage be as smooth as the gentle ripples on its immaculate waters.

Transportation Options

As you set your eyes on the gorgeous vistas of Lake Como, the trip becomes as important as the destination itself. Navigate the magical universe of transportation alternatives, where each form of travel uncovers a new side of the region's splendor. In this book, we prepare the road for your flawless voyage around Lake Como.

1. Arriving in Milan:

Gateway to Lake Como: Milan serves as the principal entrance to Lake Como, with Milan Malpensa Airport (MXP) being the biggest international airport in the area. Consider arriving in Milan and then travelling further to the lake.

Alternative Airports: Other airports, such as Milan Linate Airport (LIN) and Bergamo Orio al Serio Airport (BGY), also give connectivity to the area. Choose the airport that best corresponds with your trip plans.

2. Lake Como by Train:

Scenic Rail Journeys: Boarding a train from Milan to Lake Como is not only a source of transportation; it's an entire experience. The train ride expands through stunning landscapes, affording vistas of attractive villages and the turquoise expanse of the lake.

Central train Stations: Como San Giovanni and Varenna-Esino are the principal train stations on Lake Como. Depending on your destination, you may select the station that best matches your schedule.

3. Boating Bliss:

Lake Como Ferries: Embrace the romanticism of Lake Como by traveling its waters on a ferry. The network of ferries links major towns, giving a relaxing and picturesque means of transit.

Private Boat Rentals: For a more personal encounter, try hiring a private boat. Explore quiet coves, old homes, and secret places at your own speed.

4. Road Tripping Magic:

Scenic Drives: Lake Como is a heaven for road excursions. Navigate the winding roads around the lake, enjoying stunning views of the water and neighboring mountains. Consider hiring a vehicle for the flexibility to explore at your leisure.

 Public Transportation: An excellent bus network runs around Lake Como, giving a handy and cost-effective alternative for touring cities and villages.

5. Cable Cars and Funiculars:

Ascending Heights: Enhance your Lake Como experience by riding cable cars or funiculars to lofty overlooks. From Brunate to Pigra, these travel alternatives provide panoramic perspectives of the lake and its environs.

6. Biking Adventures:

Cycling Trails: Embrace the outdoors by touring Lake Como on two wheels. Scenic bicycle routes crisscross through quaint towns and lakeside walks, giving an energetic and engaging way to enjoy the area.

7. Practical Tips for Transportation:

Timetables & Schedules: Familiarize yourself with transit times, particularly for trains and ferries, to organise your route successfully.

Ticketing Options: Explore ticketing alternatives that meet your travel requirements, whether it's single-journey tickets, day passes, or multi-day packages.

Weather Considerations:Be wary of weather conditions, particularly if you intend on going by boat. Lake Como's weather might effect transit scheduling.

Crafting Your Travel Symphony:

Your voyage around Lake Como is not only a transfer from point A to B; it's a symphony of experiences, each transportation method contributing its particular notes to the song of your discovery. As you traverse the beaches of this Italian treasure, may your transportation options enhance the charm of Lake Como and become a vital part of your trip story.

Chapter 3: Exploring Lake Como

Overview of Lake Como

Nestled like a sapphire diamond in the midst of Lombardy, Italy, Lake Como stands as a tribute to the incredible beauty given upon Earth. As you begin on this visual voyage, prepare to immerse yourself in the appeal of a spot where nature's grandeur meets human beauty in a magnificent dance along the water's edge.

1. The Azure Symphony:

Geographical Splendor: Lake Como, with its stunning Y-shaped length, encompasses around 146 square kilometers, cradled by the embrace of the pre-Alpine Alps. Its blue waters reflect the surrounding peaks, producing a gorgeous symphony that varies with the light of the sun.

Botanical Beauty: Surrounding the lake, verdant gardens and flowering landscapes offer a touch of floral magnificence. Villas with groomed lawns, such as Villa Carlotta and Villa Balbianello, further accentuate the natural canvas.

2. Towns and Villages Along the Shores:

Bellagio - The Pearl of the Lake: As you traverse the coastlines, each hamlet exposes a distinct character. Bellagio, frequently touted as the gem of Lake Como, enchants with its cobblestone alleys, antique homes, and magnificent vistas.

Como - Where Elegance Resides: The namesake town of Como exhibits a perfect combination of medieval and Renaissance architecture. Its waterfront promenade, dotted with cafés and stores, is an invitation to leisurely strolls.

Varenna - Tranquility Personified: Varenna, on the eastern coast, emanates serenity. Its colorful buildings, lakeshore walkways, and the old Vezio Castle provide a quiet respite.

3. Historical Tapestry:

Villas and Palaces: Lake Como is dotted with antique mansions and castles that relate stories of luxury. Villa del Balbianello, with its tiered gardens, and Villa Olmo, exhibiting neoclassical grandeur, exist as living monuments of a bygone period.

The Ancient Essence: Explore the medieval splendour of towns like Bellano and Argegno, whose cobblestone alleys and historic cathedrals transport you to another time.

4. Culinary Soiree:

Gastronomic Elegance: Lake Como is not simply a scenic feast; it's a gourmet extravaganza. Indulge in genuine Italian cuisine at lakeside trattorias and Michelin-starred eateries. From risotto to lake fish, every meal is a celebration of local ingredients.

Wine and Dine with a View: Lakeside eating becomes an experience in itself. Imagine eating wonderful foods while the sun sets over the river, throwing a golden light over the surrounding hills.

5. Cultural Reverie:

Local Festivals: Immerse yourself in the cultural tapestry of Lake Como by visiting local events. From the Como Film Festival to the Palio del Baradello, these events lend energy to the area.

Artistic Flourish: Explore museums and art galleries reflecting the rich artistic legacy of the region. The Silk Museum in Como and the Civic Art Gallery in Bellagio are cultural gems waiting to be found.

6. Natural Adventures:

Boating Bliss: Lake Como's crystal-clear waters urge exploration. Hop on a ferry, charter a private boat, or go on a sailing excursion to explore secret coves, lovely towns, and ancient homes from the sea.

Scenic Hiking Trails: For nature aficionados, the nearby hills provide excellent hiking paths. From the Greenway del Lago to the Sentiero del Viandante, these routes expose magnificent vistas of the lake and beyond.

7. Seasonal Symphony:

Spring Blossoms: In April, the lake is decked with blooms. Gardens explode into color, producing a colourful tapestry that matches the growing warmth.

Summer Bliss: Summer turns Lake Como into a playground. Boating, swimming, and lakeside promenades become the order of the day, as the area basks in the sun's golden radiance.

Autumn's Palette: As fall comes, the greenery around the lake changes into a pallet of warm colours. Tranquility returns, giving a great environment for introspection.

Winter Elegance: Winter gives a peaceful appeal. Snow-capped peaks and holiday lights along the lakeside provide an exquisite touch to the environment.

Crafting Your Lake Como Tale:

As you sink into the embrace of Lake Como, consider yourself as part of a timeless tale authored by nature, enhanced by history, and ornamented with the beauty of Italian culture. Let each town, each house, and each gastronomic pleasure become a chapter in your particular novel of Lake Como, a location where fantasies are sewn into the fabric of reality.

Welcome to a world where beauty has no boundaries, and every moment is a brushstroke on the canvas of your extraordinary adventure.

Towns and Villages Around the Lake

Embark on a tour along the shores of Lake Como, where each town and hamlet is a chapter in a riveting narrative. From the timeless beauty of Bellagio to the serene embrace of Varenna, let this book carry you through the stunning tapestry of settlements that decorate the lake's shore.

1. Bellagio: The Pearl of Lake Como

Elegance Personified: Bellagio, frequently touted as the gem of Lake Como, is a marvel of beauty and refinement. Its cobblestone alleys, lined with stores and cafés, weave past antique buildings, creating an aura of timeless beauty.

Gardens of Serenity: Explore the magnificent gardens of Villa Melzi and Villa Serbelloni, where the aroma of blossoming flowers mingles with panoramic views of the lake. These floral havens bring a touch of lyrical beauty to Bellagio.

Lakefront Grandeur: The lakefront promenade is a showpiece of magnificence. From lakefront restaurants to stunning vistas, every step exposes a fresh perspective of Lake Como's blue vastness.

2. Como: Where History Meets Modernity

Historical Enclave: Como town is a combination of medieval beauty and contemporary attractiveness. The Cathedral of Como, with its Gothic and Renaissance components, remains as a tribute to the town's historical prominence.

Lakeside Sophistication: The lakeside promenade is a vibrant centre, where cafés, shops, and gelaterias entice you to indulge in the art of dolce far niente (the pleasure of doing nothing).

Silk Heritage: Dive into Como's heritage as a silk-producing hub at the Silk Museum. Learn about the beautiful artistry that has graced the area for ages.

3. Varenna: Tranquil Retreat by the Water

Lakeside Simplicity: Varenna, positioned on the eastern beach, radiates calm. The colorful homes along the shoreline form a lovely landscape, encouraging leisurely strolls and periods of introspection.

Vezio Castle: Ascend to Vezio Castle for magnificent views of Lake Como. The medieval fortification gives a touch of history to Varenna and provides a wonderful vantage point to absorb the surrounding splendour.

Villa Monastero: Explore the grounds of Villa Monastero, a former Cistercian cloister turned aristocratic house. The villa's floral landscape and lakeside location make a tranquil respite.

4. Menaggio: Lakeside Bliss with Alpine Views

Piazza Garibaldi: Menaggio's center plaza, Piazza Garibaldi, is a busy hub surrounded by cafés and businesses. The ideal setting to drink an espresso while taking in the lakeside scenery.

Lido di Menaggio: Enjoy lakeside tranquility at Lido di Menaggio, a seaside location featuring a pool, beach, and breathtaking views. It's a great spot to relax and revel in the splendor of Lake Como.

Alpine Adventures: Use Menaggio as a starting point for exploring the nearby hills. The adjacent Monte Grona and Rifugio Menaggio provide hiking paths with beautiful alpine vistas.

5. Tremezzo: Elegance and Grandeur

Villa Carlotta: Tremezzo is home to the magnificence of house Carlotta, an 18th-century house surrounded by floral gardens. Marvel at the art collections, lush flora, and views of Bellagio from the villa's terraces.

The Greenway del Lago: Embark on the Greenway del Lago, a lovely walking path linking Tremezzo to Griante and Colonno. The walk gives sights of both the lake and the neighboring hills.

Grand Hotel Tremezzo: Experience luxury at the Grand Hotel Tremezzo, a famous lakeside resort. Indulge in lakeside meals, wellness treatments, and the luxury of a bygone period.

Crafting Your Lakeside Symphony:

Lake Como's cities and villages are not simply destinations; they are experiences waiting to be experienced. Each town, with its own character and offers, adds to the symphony of beauty that distinguishes Lake Como. As you travel the shoreline, let each cobblestone street, lakeside scenery, and cultural jewel become a note in the tune of your lakeside symphony. Welcome to a trip where every town tells a tale, and every hamlet asks you to be part of the magic that is Lake Como.

Historical Significance

Lake Como, beyond its amazing beauty, contains within its grasp a tapestry weaved with centuries of history. As you explore through its cities and along its coasts, you enter into a place where ancient echoes and lavish legacies combine, creating a tale that transcends time.

1. Ancient Beginnings:

Etruscan and Roman Legacy: Lake Como's history extends back to Etruscan times, with traces of old villages and trade routes. The Romans, understanding the strategic and scenic significance of the area, erected villas and trade stations along the coasts.

Pliny the Younger: The Roman historian Pliny the Younger, fascinated by the lake's splendor, owned a home in Como. His writings beautifully depict the sceneries and leisurely hobbies enjoyed on the beaches of Lake Como during the 1st century.

2. Medieval Charms:

Como Cathedral (Duomo): The Como Cathedral, a remarkable combination of Gothic and Renaissance architecture, serves as a tribute to the medieval workmanship of the area. Its development spans decades, resulting in a masterwork that compels tourists to marvel at its meticulous features.

Ancient Walls and Towers: Towns like Como and Bellano are ornamented with vestiges of medieval defenses, including historic walls and towers. These monuments serve as quiet testament to the strategic significance of Lake Como throughout history.

3. Renaissance Opulence:

Villa del Balbianello: Built in the late 18th century on the western coast of Lake Como, Villa del Balbianello typifies Renaissance luxury. The villa's tiered grounds, filled with sculptures and fountains, provide a peek into the opulent lifestyle of its past aristocratic owners.

Villa Carlotta: Constructed in the late 17th century, Villa Carlotta shows the neoclassical grandeur of the period. Its art collections and floral gardens represent the cultural aspirations and sophisticated tastes of the nobility.

4. Silk and Trade Prosperity:

Como: Silk Capital: In the 19th century, Como evolved as a worldwide hub for silk manufacture. The city's Silk Museum chronicles the narrative of Como's supremacy in the silk trade, stressing the skill and invention that powered its wealth.

Trade Routes and Commerce: Lake Como's strategic location encouraged trade routes and commerce, contributing to the region's economic expansion. The villages along the seashore prospered as sites of cultural interchange and commercial activity.

5. Celebrity Retreats and Modern Allure:

Villa Oleandra and Celebrity Presence: In recent times, Lake Como has been a magnet for celebrities and dignitaries. Villa Oleandra in Laglio, owned by George Clooney, is a noteworthy example. The lake's attraction has made it a getaway for individuals seeking both natural beauty and a feeling of tranquility.

Modern Cultural Events: Lake Como continues to be a cultural hotspot, holding events like the Como Film Festival. These modern festivals provide a contemporary element to the region's historical importance, ensuring that Lake Como remains a thriving cultural attraction.

6. Resilience and Timeless Allure:

Enduring through Wars: Lake Como, with its strategic significance, saw the turmoil of wars and battles. Despite the hardships, the area has stayed strong, conserving its cultural richness and natural beauties.

Timeless Beauty: The historical importance of Lake Como resides not only in its history but in its capacity to perfectly mix the old with the present. As you explore the shoreline, the ageless charm of the lake begs you to become part of its eternal tale.

Crafting Your Historical Odyssey:

Lake Como's history is not a static narrative; it's a dynamic trip that unfolds with each step along its shoreline. As you visit the cities, villas, and cultural treasures, may you experience the echoes of ages past and admire the perseverance that has formed Lake Como into the timeless beauty it is today. Welcome to a spot where history whispers through every cobblestone and dances in the reflection of the turquoise waters—a place where the past and present combine in an endless symphony.

Local Culture and Traditions

Lake Como, decorated with natural beauty, is also a living canvas painted with the bright colors of local culture and customs. As you immerse yourself in the rhythm of lakeside life, you'll find a town strongly anchored in its tradition, where every celebration, artisan craft, and gastronomic treat recounts a narrative handed down through generations.

1. Passion for Festivals:

Palio del Baradello: Join the locals in celebrating the famous Palio del Baradello in Como. This medieval festival, replete with costumed processions and historical contests, takes you to a bygone period, mirroring the atmosphere of friendship and tradition.

Sagra di San Giovanni: Experience the Sagra di San Giovanni in Bellagio, a celebration devoted to the patron saint of the town. Amidst colorful processions, music, and fireworks, you'll observe the deep-seated religious and community relationships.

2. Artisanal Craftsmanship:

Silk Weaving Heritage: Como's past as a silk-producing powerhouse comes to life in the complex motifs of locally woven silk. Visit artisan workshops to experience the workmanship behind Como silk, where traditions of pattern-making and weaving are kept with pride.

Woodworking Traditions: In lakeside settlements, traditional woodworking thrives. Handcrafted wooden products, from elaborate sculptures to artisan furniture, reflect the expertise and passion of local artisans.

3. Culinary Traditions:

Polenta and Fish Delights: Lake Como's culinary traditions are a feast for the senses. Indulge in local specialties like "missultin," sun-dried fish from Lake Como, coupled with creamy polenta. These recipes show a delicate combination of lake-sourced ingredients and Alpine tastes.

Crotti Experience: Explore the distinctive Crotti, traditional cellars cut into the hillside, where villagers congregate for convivial meals. The Crotti experience gives a taste of local cheeses, cured meats, and wines, all within a friendly, communal atmosphere.

4. Lakeside Markets:

Como's Market Day: Immerse yourself in the exciting atmosphere of Como's market day. Stroll among vendors stocked with fresh food, specialty cheeses, and local crafts. It's a sensory trip that links you with the pulse of everyday life around the lake.

Varenna's Local Markets: In Varenna, local markets give an insight into the community's agricultural heritage. From seasonal vegetables to homemade goods, these marketplaces exhibit the richness of local skills.

5. Maritime Traditions:

Nautical Heritage: Lake Como's maritime traditions are honored in events like the Palio Remiero del Lario. Witness rowing events that highlight the historical role of boats in commerce and transportation on the lake.

Sailing Festivals: Sailing events, such as the Centomiglia regatta, gather fans from throughout the globe. The sight of sailboats delicately sailing the lake bears respect to the maritime past of Lake Como.

6. Music and Performing Arts:

Villa Erba Concerts: Attend open-air performances at Villa Erba, where the tones of classical music mingle with the natural surroundings. These cultural events demonstrate Lake Como as a site where creative traditions are recognised and honored.

Como's Teatro Sociale: Step inside Como's Teatro Sociale, a historic theater featuring a variety of shows. From opera to modern plays, the theater symbolizes the everlasting interest for the performing arts in the area.

7. Sustainability and Environmental Stewardship:

Green Initiatives: Lake Como's villages are actively involved in sustainability measures. Initiatives like as eco-friendly tourism, trash reduction, and environmental conservation programmes reflect a dedication to maintaining the natural grandeur of the area.

Local Advocacy: Join local efforts promoting environmental concerns, such as cleanup projects around the lake shoreline. These activities illustrate the intimate link between the people and the preservation of Lake Como's natural beauty.

Crafting Your Cultural Odyssey:

Lake Como's local culture and customs are not merely vestiges of the past; they are a live, breathing representation of a community proud of its history. As you visit the villages, mingle with residents, and appreciate the flavors of heritage, may you become a part of the continuing story that makes Lake Como a cultural treasure trove. Welcome to a location where every tradition is an invitation to interact, and every ethnic detail adds a layer to the rich tapestry that is Lake Como.

Chapter 4: Accommodations

Hotels, Resorts, and Boutique Stays

Lake Como, with its stunning scenery and historic appeal, provides a range of lodgings that surpasses conventional stays—they are experiences in themselves. From opulent hotels to quaint boutique getaways, let this book expose you to the richness and peace that lie in the embrace of Lake Como.

1. Grand Hotel Tremezzo: A Lakeside Oasis

Timeless Elegance: Grand Hotel Tremezzo, a 5-star jewel, combines old-world elegance with a dash of contemporary grandeur. Overlooking Bellagio, this ancient hotel has magnificent decor, verdant gardens, and a floating pool on the lake—a veritable refuge of pleasure.

La Terrazza Gualtiero Marchesi: Immerse yourself in gastronomic brilliance at the hotel's Michelin-starred restaurant. With magnificent lake views, the dining experience is a symphony of tastes created by Chef Gualtiero Marchesi.

2. Villa d'Este: A Palatial Retreat

Palatial Grandeur: Mansion d'Este in Cernobbio is a famous 16th-century mansion converted 5-star hotel. Surrounded by 25 acres of grounds, the hotel radiates enormous magnificence. Each room is a monument to ageless grandeur and refinement.

Michelin-Starred Dining: Experience gastronomic pleasures at the hotel's Michelin-starred restaurants. Whether eating at the Veranda or Grill, each meal is a gourmet excursion that compliments the royal setting.

3. Il Sereno Lago di Como: Contemporary Chic

Modern Sophistication: Il Sereno Lago di Como, a contemporary 5-star hotel in Torno, harmoniously integrates modern design with the natural splendor of Lake Como. Floor-to-ceiling windows, private patios, and elegant decor define the spirit of this boutique getaway.

Michelin-Starred Berton Al Lago: Indulge in contemporary Italian food at the hotel's Berton Al Lago restaurant, helmed by Chef Andrea Berton. The culinary masterpieces, along with lake vistas, create a gourmet spectacular.

4. CastaDiva Resort & Spa: Lakeside Serenity

Historic Elegance: CastaDiva Resort & Spa, set on the banks Lake Blevio, evokes the spirit of lakeside calm. Housed in a former mansion of opera star Giuditta Pasta, the resort blends historic grandeur and contemporary sophistication.

Private Villas: For an intimate escape, choose for one of the resort's private villas, complete with exclusive access to the lake, gardens, and customized services.

5. Mandarin Oriental, Lake Como: Asian-Inspired Bliss

Harmonious Retreat: Mandarin Oriental, Lake Como, provides a splash of Asian-inspired elegance to the lakeshore. Set in a magnificent 18th-century palace, the resort provides large accommodations, verdant gardens, and spectacular lake views.

Wellness Haven: Rejuvenate at the resort's spa center, where holistic therapies, a Turkish bath, and an indoor pool provide a refuge for relaxation.

6. Relais Villa Vittoria: Boutique Charm
Intimate Elegance: Relais Villa Vittoria in Laglio is a boutique hotel that symbolizes intimate elegance. With just 11 rooms, the environment is unique and individualized, giving a tranquil vacation on the lake.

Panoramic Terrace and Infinity Pool: Revel in breathtaking lake views from the hotel's balcony and infinity pool. It's a refuge of solitude surrounded by the lush vegetation of the hills.

7. Filario Hotel & Residences: Contemporary Comfort

Modern Retreat: Filario Hotel & Residences in Lezzeno provides modern luxury against the background of Lake Como. The hotel's simple architecture, large rooms, and lakefront access make a great balance of modernism and natural beauty.

Private Lakeside Deck: Select a house with a private lakefront terrace to relish unrestricted views and direct access to the crystal-clear waters of the lake.

Crafting Your Lakeside Escape:

Lake Como's hotels are not merely somewhere to rest; they are extensions of the destination's attraction. As you pick your hideaway on the lake, may each hotel, resort, or boutique stay become a chapter in your lakeside story—a private getaway where the beauty of Lake Como perfectly intertwines with the luxury of your surroundings. Welcome to a world where extravagance meets calm, and every stay is a celebration of the everlasting wonder that is Lake Como.

Accommodation Recommendations by Budget

Lake Como, a world of unsurpassed beauty, provides a variety of lodgings that suit to diverse budgets. Whether you seek luxury retreats, lovely mid-range havens, or budget-friendly jewels, let this guide design your lakeside experience, ensuring every stay becomes a harmonising note in your Lake Como symphony.

Luxury Retreats:

1. Grand Hotel Tremezzo

A Symphony of Opulence: Grand Hotel Tremezzo, a 5-star hideaway, mixes history and elegance flawlessly. With breathtaking lake views, elegant decor, and Michelin-starred food, it's an opulent sanctuary where each moment is a crescendo of delight.

2. Villa d'Este

Palatial Grandeur: palace d'Este, a famous 16th-century palace turned 5-star hotel, draws you into a realm of magnificent splendour. Set among wide grounds, the apartments ooze timeless elegance, creating a royal ambiance.

3. Il Sereno Lago di Como

Contemporary Chic: Il Sereno Lago di Como, a contemporary 5-star hideaway, provides elegant design against the background of Lake Como's grandeur. The Michelin-starred Berton Al Lago restaurant and private patios heighten the experience.

Mid-Range Gems:

1. CastaDiva Resort & Spa

Lakeside Serenity: CastaDiva Resort & Spa, merging historic elegance and contemporary comforts, offers an exquisite lakeside vacation. The private villas and spa give peace among the verdant surroundings.

2. Relais Villa Vittoria

Boutique Intimacy: Relais Villa Vittoria, a boutique hotel in Laglio, emanates intimate elegance. With a limited number of accommodations, individual service, and panoramic views, it's a tranquil refuge on Lake Como.

3. Filario Hotel & Residences

Contemporary Comfort: Filario Hotel & Residences in Lezzeno provides a contemporary hideaway with lakefront access. Spacious rooms, simple décor, and a private lakeside porch make a great combination of comfort and flair.

Budget-Friendly Gems:

1. Albergo Terminus

Como Town Charm: Albergo Terminus in Como town provides budget-friendly lodging without sacrificing on charm. Its central position offers easy investigation of the town's historical landmarks.

2. Hotel Centrale Bellagio

Bellagio's Affordability: Hotel Centrale Bellagio offers budget-friendly lodgings in the center of Bellagio. Its strategic position gives easy access to the town's attractions and the ferry station.

3. Hotel Villa Cipressi

Varenna's Affordable Gem: Hotel Villa Cipressi in Varenna mixes affordability with lakefront beauty. The hotel's grounds, closeness to the lake, and historic atmosphere make it a lovely budget alternative.

Traveler's Tips:

Advance Bookings: For premium and mid-range lodgings, consider reserving in advance, particularly during busy seasons, to get the greatest pricing and availability.

Off-Peak Exploration: Budget-conscious tourists may discover fantastic prices during the off-peak seasons (spring and autumn), allowing for a more cost-effective lakeside vacation.

Local Experiences: Engage with the local culture by discovering budget-friendly activities, such as wandering through markets, enjoying lakeside promenades, and experiencing real street cuisine.

Crafting Your Lakeside Symphony:

Lake Como welcomes every budget with open arms, providing a selection of lodgings that appeal to various interests. Whether you pick luxury, mid-range, or budget-friendly lodgings, each lodge becomes a major note in your lakeside symphony. Embrace the customized peacefulness of Lake Como, where your selected refuge is not only a place to stay but a vital part of your wonderful lakeside tale.

Unique Stay Experiences

Lake Como, a canvas of beauty, also uncovers unique stay experiences that surpass the commonplace. From ancient villas to lovely eco-retreats, let this book take you into a world where every stay becomes a personalized chapter in your lakeside voyage.

1. Villa Balbiano: Timeless Opulence

Historical Grandeur: estate Balbiano, a beautiful 16th-century estate near Ossuccio, provides premium accommodations in a setting of timeless splendor. With its frescoed ceilings, magnificent grounds, and private boat access, this house immerses visitors in the grandeur of Lake Como's noble past.

2. Casa sull'Albero: Treehouse Retreat

Elevated Tranquility: Experience Lake Como from new heights at Casa sull'Albero, a treehouse hidden in the hills of Argegno. With panoramic views and a combination of contemporary comforts with rustic charm, this unique refuge provides a memorable getaway.

3. Como Casa: Floating Glamping

Aquatic Adventure: Como Casa, a floating glamping experience, enables you to sleep on the peaceful waters of Lake Como. These floating cottages, situated near the town of Lecco, provide a creative way to interact with the lake, with the calming sounds of water lulling you to sleep.

4. Eremo Gaudio: Cliffside Sanctuary

Secluded Splendor: Eremo Gaudio, a cliffside hermitage in Varenna, provides a private retreat with panoramic views of the lake. This unusual residence, located on the brink of a cliff, offers for a close touch with nature in a setting of tranquil beauty.

5. Casa del Portico: Historic Charm

Medieval Elegance: Casa del Portico, situated in the historic town of Nesso, is a lovely property with a covered portico overlooking the lake. Immerse yourself in the historical environment of our unique hotel, where each stone tells stories from the past.

6. I Tigli in Theoria: Culinary Retreat

Gastronomic Bliss: I Tigli in Theoria, situated in the town of Como, combines a Michelin-starred restaurant with luxury apartments. Delight in a gourmet getaway where the art of cuisine meets the luxury of sumptuous lodgings in this unique blend of tastes and comfort.

7. Vista Palazzo Lago di Como: Urban Sophistication

City Retreat: Vista Palazzo Lago di Como, located in the centre of Como town, elegantly mixes urban refinement with lakeside beauty. This boutique hotel provides a unique stay experience where the excitement of the town meets the calm of the lake.

Traveler's Tips:

bespoke Experiences: Engage with your accommodation's concierge to design unique experiences, whether it's a private boat excursion, a bespoke culinary lesson, or a tailored spa getaway.

Off-Beat Exploration: Venture beyond the well-trodden trails and discover the lesser-known nooks of Lake Como. Unique stays frequently come with the extra bonus of finding hidden treasures in the area.

Seasonal Sensations: Consider the season while arranging your visit. From flowering spring gardens to winter's warm charm, Lake Como's various lodgings provide different experiences dependent on the time of year.

Crafting Your Bespoke Lake Como Tale:

Lake Como's distinctive stay experiences are invited to delve into a world where every aspect is meticulously planned, and each moment becomes an immersive vacation. As you select from medieval homes, treehouse retreats, or floating glamping, may your stay be a canvas for unique memories, merging the remarkable with the tranquil in the heart of this Italian beauty. Welcome to a place where individuality is not just a feature; it's the fundamental core of your lakeside experience.

Chapter 5: Dining and Culinary Delights

Traditional Italian Cuisine

Embark on a culinary adventure into the heart of Italy as we explore the rich tapestry of traditional Italian food. From the sun-kissed sands of the Amalfi Coast to the rolling hills of Tuscany and the timeless elegance of Rome, each area adds its distinct characteristics, producing a symphony of taste that transcends boundaries.

Antipasti: Prelude to Pleasure

1. Bruschetta al Pomodoro:

Tomato Elegance: Savor the simplicity of Bruschetta al Pomodoro—a song of juicy tomatoes, fresh basil, garlic, and extra virgin olive oil over toasted bread. It's a flavor of summer wrapped in a single mouthful.

2. Prosciutto e Melone:

Sweet and Savory Ballet: Prosciutto e Melone orchestrates a tango between sweet melon and finely sliced prosciutto. The contrast of flavors—sweet, salty, and savory—is a timeless composition.

3. Caprese Salad:

Mozzarella Serenade: Caprese Salad, a salute to the colors of the Italian flag, blends fresh mozzarella, luscious tomatoes, and basil. Drizzled with olive oil, it's a lovely homage to simplicity.

Primi Piatti: Pasta Perfection

4. Risotto alla Milanese:
Saffron Sonata: Risotto alla Milanese, born in the heart of Lombardy, is a creamy masterpiece. Saffron-infused Arborio rice produces a golden symphony, complemented by the richness of Parmesan cheese.

5. Spaghetti Carbonara:

Roman Elegance: Spaghetti Carbonara, a Roman classic, harmonizes eggs, Pecorino Romano cheese, pancetta, and black pepper. Its silky texture and powerful tastes commemorate the art of Roman culinary simplicity.

6. Orecchiette alle Cime di Rapa:

Puglian Delight: Orecchiette alle Cime di Rapa from Puglia blends "little ears" pasta with broccoli rabe, garlic, and chili flakes. It's a monument to the geographical variety that distinguishes Italian food.

Secondi Piatti: Symphony of Mains

7. Osso Buco:

Milanese Comfort: Osso Buco, a Milanese staple, contains braised veal shanks in a rich broth of white wine, broth, and tomatoes. Gremolata—a blend of lemon zest, garlic, and parsley—adds a zesty flare.

8. Saltimbocca alla Romana:

Roman Delight: Saltimbocca alla Romana, a Roman delicacy, highlights veal escalopes topped with prosciutto and sage. Pan-seared to perfection, it's a meal that encapsulates the spirit of Roman culinary refinement.

9. Branzino al Cartoccio:

Seafood Symphony: Branzino al Cartoccio, a seafood mixture from coastal areas, comprises Mediterranean sea bass cooked with herbs, cherry tomatoes, and olives in parchment paper. The outcome is a subtle balance of tastes.

Contorni: Harmonious Sides

10. Insalata di Rucola e Parmigiano:

Peppery Refrain: Insalata di Rucola e Parmigiano, a spicy arugula salad garnished with shavings of Parmesan cheese, offers a delightful break between dishes.

11. Caponata:

Sicilian Symphony: Caponata, a Sicilian eggplant dish, includes eggplant, tomatoes, olives, and capers. Sweet and acidic tones dance together in a symphony of Sicilian tastes.

Dolci: Sweet Crescendo

12. Tiramisu:

Coffee Euphoria: Tiramisu, the crescendo of every Italian supper, combines coffee-soaked ladyfingers with mascarpone and chocolate. Its moniker, meaning "pick me up," appropriately encapsulates the joy it generates.

13. Cannoli Siciliani:

Sicilian Epiphany: Cannoli Siciliani, Sicily's gift to the sweet taste, contains crispy pastry tubes filled with ricotta and sweet treats. Each mouthful is a marvel of texture and taste.

Digestivi: A Closing Refrain

14. Limoncello:
Citrus Cadence: Conclude your Italian feast with Limoncello, a lemon liqueur from the Amalfi Coast. Its zesty undertones bring a pleasant ending to your gastronomic trip.

Wine Pairing: Vinous Overture

Chianti Classico: Enhance pasta recipes with the powerful flavors of a Chianti Classico from Tuscany.

Barolo: Pair Osso Buco or substantial meats with the assertiveness of a Barolo from Piedmont.

Vermentino: Complement seafood meals with the freshness of a Vermentino from Sardinia.

Crafting Your Italian Epicurean Tale:

Traditional Italian food is not only a meal; it's a symphony that resonates with the essence of each area. As you appreciate the different flavors and textures, may your gastronomic adventure around Italy be a rich tapestry of tastes—a feast that mirrors the love, history, and passion that characterise this timeless cuisine. Buon appetito!

Popular Local Dishes

Lake Como, with its magnificent views, has a gastronomic repertoire that complements the richness of its surroundings. From the waters of Bellagio to the small towns like Varenna, each region lends its distinctive notes to the gourmet song. Let's start on a scrumptious tour through the famous local delicacies that characterize the culinary uniqueness of Lake Como.

1. Missoltino: The Lake's Bounty

Dish Harmony: Missoltino is a classic dish incorporating sun-dried and salted fish, generally obtained from Lake Como. Grilled to perfection, it's a celebration of the lake's riches with a unique preservation technique.

2. Risotto al Pesce Persico: Freshwater Elegance

Lakeside Euphony: Risotto al Pesce Persico is a compelling meal that showcases perch, a freshwater fish plentiful in Lake Como. The subtle tastes of the fish infiltrate the creamy risotto, producing a harmony of taste.

3. Polenta e Misultin: Alpine Harmony

Culinary Crescendo: Polenta e Misultin displays the perfect coupling of polenta, a classic in Italian cuisine, with Misultin—small, dried fish from Lake Como. The dish reflects the region's Alpine and lakefront elements.

4. Lavarello with Polenta: Lakeside Symphony

Melody of Flavors: Lavarello con Polenta contains lavarello, a whitefish endemic to Lake Como, served atop creamy polenta. The meal encapsulates the spirit of lakeside dining, where the freshest catch meets rustic comfort.

5. Pizzoccheri di Valtellina: Mountain Melange

Valtellina Serenade: While not immediately on Lake Como, Pizzoccheri della Valtellina is a mountainous pleasure close. Buckwheat pasta is coupled with cabbage, potatoes, and local cheese, producing a meal that embodies the alpine traditions of the area.

6. Formaggini di Tremosine: Cheesy Refrain

Melting Melody: Formaggi di Tremosine highlights little cheese rounds made in the Tremosine area. These semi-soft cheeses are commonly served with local bread, producing a symphony of creamy textures.

7. Tiramisu al Limoncello: Citrus Crescendo

Lemon-infused Delight: A regional version, Tiramisu al Limoncello, combines the original Tiramisu with the zesty flavors of Limoncello—a lemon liqueur from the surrounding Amalfi Coast. It's a beautiful crescendo that evokes the sense of Italian gluttony.

8. Gelato di Mandorla: Nutty Serenade

Nutty Bliss: Gelato di Mandorla is an almond-flavored gelato that adorns the beaches of Lake Como. The smooth, nutty undertones give a welcome break on a warm lakeside day.

9. Panettone: Festive Anthem

Seasonal Extravaganza: While historically linked with Christmas, Panettone is a festive delicacy eaten throughout the year. The sweet bread, loaded with candied fruits and raisins, lends a touch of festivity to Lake Como's culinary repertoire.

10. Crodino: Bittersweet Intermezzo

Aperitivo Elegance: Crodino is a non-alcoholic aperitif that provides a bittersweet intermezzo to lakeside dining. Served over ice with a slice of orange, it's a popular option for those wanting a refreshing pre-dinner drink.

Crafting Your Culinary Sonata:

Lake Como's famed local dishes are more than meals; they are a melodious voyage through the tastes of the area. As you eat each meal, may you experience the rhythm of the lake, the embrace of the mountains, and the ethnic subtleties that make every mouthful a symphony of flavor. Buon Appetito

Fine Dining and Casual Eateries

Lake Como's culinary landscape is a beautiful combination of refinement and simplicity, where sophisticated dining places and charming informal diners converge to create a symphony of tastes. From sophisticated lakefront restaurants to small trattorias buried in mediaeval alleys, let's discover the culinary jewels that appeal to both discriminating palates and those seeking the pleasure of informal eating.

Fine Dining Extravaganza:

1. Ristorante Silvio:

Lakeside Opulence: Nestled in Bellagio, Ristorante Silvio provides a great dining experience with a spectacular view of Lake Como. Immerse yourself in an evening of gourmet delight, with expertly designed meals that highlight the region's best ingredients.

2. Il Gatto Nero:

Historic Elegance: Il Gatto Nero in Cernobbio blends traditional beauty with gourmet quality. Set in a centuries-old edifice, the restaurant's fine dining cuisine includes a combination of classic and creative foods, offering a feast for the senses.

3. Mistral:

Contemporary Delight: Mistral, situated in the Grand Hotel Villa Serbelloni in Bellagio, provides a contemporary version of Italian food. With a Michelin-starred chef at the lead, Mistral's cuisine is a gastronomic adventure that embraces the region's delicacies with creative flare.

4. La Veranda:

Riverside Romance: La Veranda at the Villa d'Este in Cernobbio delivers an amazing fine dining experience along the shores of Lake Como. The restaurant's patio offers a perfect environment to appreciate gastronomic delights while surrounded by the beauty of the home and its grounds.

5. I Tigli in Theoria:

Gastronomic Symphony: Tigli in Theoria, situated in Como, perfectly integrates a Michelin-starred restaurant with an artistic setting. The inventive food, along with a comprehensive wine selection, welcomes customers on a culinary voyage via exquisite sensations.

Casual Eateries Serenade:

1. Trattoria Baita Belvedere:

Mountain Retreat: Trattoria Baita Belvedere, located in the hills near Bellagio, provides a rural getaway with a casual but lovely ambiance. Delight in traditional meals, such as pasta and local fish, while surrounded by the peacefulness of nature.

2. Ristorante La Punta:

Lakeside Simplicity: Ristorante La Punta in Varenna retains the charm of informal lakeside dining. Overlooking the lake, the restaurant encourages customers to experience basic but delectable food, such as freshly caught fish and handmade pasta.

3. Crotto dei Platani:

Riverside Charm: Crotto dei Platani in Brienno provides a relaxed escape with a riverfront environment. Sample local delights, like lake fish and handmade pasta, in a calm setting surrounded by beautiful nature.

4. Al Veluu Ristorante:

Panoramic Delight: Al Veluu Ristorante in Tremezzo serves informal eating with a spectacular view of Lake Como. The patio, overlooking the sea and neighboring mountains, is a great setting to savor classic Italian cuisine cooked with locally sourced ingredients.

5. Trattoria del Fagiano:

Historic Whimsy: Trattoria del Fagiano in Bellagio welcomes customers to enter into a classic environment with its attractive interiors and outdoor patio. The menu provides a range of warm foods influenced by regional tastes.

Crafting Your Culinary Overture:

Lake Como's gourmet dining places and informal restaurants each provide a particular movement in the gastronomic symphony of the area. Whether you find yourself indulging in culinary delicacies or relishing the simplicity of traditional meals, may every meal along the beaches of Lake Como be a pleasant note in your lakeside adventure. Buon Appetito!

Lakefront Dining Experiences

Lakefront dining experiences on the beaches of Lake Como are a sensory feast, where gastronomic pleasures are enhanced by the soft lapping of water and panoramic views of the surrounding landscapes. Whether you desire sophisticated elegance or informal charm, Lake Como's shoreline cafés provide a gastronomic adventure that echoes with the beat of the water.

Elegant Lakefront Extravaganza:

1. Villa d'Este Floating Restaurant:
Aquatic Grandeur: The Floating Restaurant at Villa d'Este in Cernobbio is an ideal of lakeside luxury. Dine on a floating patio surrounded by the grandeur of the lake and savor in delicious delicacies that mimic the splendor of the old mansion.

2. La Terrazza Gualtiero Marchesi:

Michelin-Starred Panorama: La Terrazza Gualtiero Marchesi at Grand Hotel Tremezzo provides a Michelin-starred dining experience with a terrace overlooking Bellagio. Immerse yourself in a gastronomic masterpiece while the lake unfolds before you in all its magnificence.

3. Ristorante Bilacus:

Bellagio Bliss: Ristorante Bilacus in Bellagio captivates with its beachfront patio, affording magnificent views of the lake. The cuisine promotes regional delicacies, enabling customers to experience authentic Italian dishes amongst a lovely environment.

Casual Lakeside Serenade:

1. Albergo Ristorante Conca Azzurra:

Nesso Charm: Albergo Ristorante Conca Azzurra in Nesso delivers a simple but stunning lakeside dining experience. Enjoy handmade pasta and fresh seafood on the balcony while enjoying the peacefulness of the surroundings.

2. Ristorante La Baia:

Varenna Vibes: Ristorante La Baia in Varenna allows visitors to experience genuine Italian food at the water's edge. The informal environment allows for a leisurely dinner while enjoying the natural grandeur of Lake Como.

3. Ristorante La Darsena:

Torno Tranquility: Ristorante La Darsena in Torno offers a laid-back lakeside hideaway. Dine al fresco on the patio and experience the tastes of fresh seafood and local products while taking in the views of the calm lake.

Panoramic Lakeside Delight:

1. Borgo Antico:

Argegno Atmosphere: Borgo Antico in Argegno provides a magnificent lakefront patio with views reaching over Lake Como. This quaint café provides a range of Italian cuisine, delivering a pleasant blend of tastes and landscape.

2. Bar Il Molo:

Lenno Lakeside Vibes: Bar Il Molo in Lenno offers a relaxing lakeside experience with an outside deck. Enjoy a selection of food, beverages, and gelato while enjoying the sunlight and the beauty of the lake.

3. La Piazzetta:

Tremezzo Terrace: La Piazzetta in Tremezzo provides a lakeside patio with views of Bellagio and the surrounding hills. The menu provides a blend of classic Italian meals and cosmopolitan tastes in a comfortable lakeside environment.

Traveler's Tips:

Sunset appointments: Consider making appointments for sunset timings to view Lake Como bathed in the warm colors of the setting sun while having a delicious supper.

Local Specialties: Embrace the local tastes by sampling meals including the catch of the day, regional cheeses, and wines made in the Lake Como area.

Seasonal Sensibilities: Lakeside eating experiences may change with the seasons, so consider the time of year to appreciate the distinct environment each season delivers.

Crafting Your Lakeside Sonata:

Lake Como's waterfront dining experiences are not only about the food; they are a celebration of the spectacular vistas and the serene mood that surrounds you. Whether you pick for exquisite fine dining or informal lakeside serenades, may each mouthful be complemented by the relaxing song of the lake, creating an enchanting gastronomic symphony by the beaches of Lake Como. Buon Appetito!

Chapter 6: Activities and Attractions

Water Activities

Lake Como, with its crystalline waters and stunning sceneries, invites you to embark on an aquatic experience. From relaxing cruises to exhilarating water sports, the lake provides a broad selection of activities that combine with the serene beauty that surrounds you. Dive into the aquatic symphony of Lake Como and let the waves become the melodies in your lakeside excursion.

1. Boat Cruises:

Lakeside Elegance: Embark on a traditional boat tour to discover Lake Como's lovely shores. Choose from private motorboats, ancient wooden boats, or beautiful yachts for a leisurely cruise. Admire the ancient homes, picturesque towns, and lush gardens that flank the lake's shore.

2. Windsurfing and Kitesurfing:

Thrills on the Breeze: If you desire an adrenaline rush, windsurfing and kitesurfing on Lake Como's waves are fantastic possibilities. The lake's constant winds make it a perfect playground for various wind-driven water activities.

3. Stand-Up Paddleboarding (SUP):

Zen on the Water: Glide over Lake Como's peaceful surface on a stand-up paddleboard. Whether you're a newbie or an expert paddler, SUP provides a calm and exciting way to interact with the lake's peacefulness.

4. Sailing:

Nautical Elegance: Set sail on Lake Como and let the wind lead you as you traverse the calm waves. Sailing classes and rentals are offered for both seasoned sailors and those wishing to experience the timeless fascination of sailing.

5. Kayaking:

Intimate Exploration: Explore secret coves, tucked-away corners, and picturesque nooks on a kayaking experience. Lake Como's tranquil waters offer a great location for kayakers of all ability levels.

6. Water Skiing:

Thrill on the Wake: Experience the pleasure of water skiing as you glide over the lake's surface. Expert instructors and rental services make it accessible for both beginners and seasoned skiers.

7. Canoeing:

Nature's Pace: Paddle at your own leisure in a canoe, enabling you to experience the natural splendor that surrounds Lake Como. Whether you select a solo excursion or a tandem experience, canoeing is a quiet way to explore.

8. Fishing:

Angler's Paradise: Lake Como is home to a diversity of fish species. Engage in the art of fishing and try your luck at catching perch, trout, or pike. Local guides can give insights into the greatest fishing places.

9. Swimming:

Refreshing Dip: During the warmer months, enjoy in a soothing dip in Lake Como's pristine waters. Many lakeside hotels and private homes have direct access to the lake, enabling you to take a swim at your leisure.

10. Hydrofoil and Seaplane Tours:

Aerial Symphony: For a new viewpoint, choose a hydrofoil or seaplane excursion that delivers stunning aerial views of Lake Como. Marvel at the stunning vista of the lake and its surrounding regions from the air.

Traveler's Tips:

Sun Protection: The sun's reflection off the sea may be strong. Bring sunscreen, a hat, and sunglasses to protect yourself from UV radiation.

Weather Awareness: Lake Como's weather might fluctuate, so be careful of wind conditions, particularly if partaking in water activities.

Local Guidance: Seek guidance from local rental operators or tour companies for the finest places and safety rules for your chosen water sport.

Crafting Your Waterside Overture:

Lake Como's water sports tempt you to immerse yourself in the aquatic symphony that distinguishes this Italian wonder. Whether you select for leisurely cruises, exhilarating water sports, or just a tranquil swim, let the lake become the canvas for your aquatic adventure—a symphony of waves and exploration on the blue canvas of Lake Como. Buon Viaggio!

Hiking and Nature Trails

Immerse yourself in the beauty of Lake Como as you explore its charming hiking and nature routes, framed by lush hills and gorgeous scenery. Each route contributes a verse to the natural symphony that adorns the coastlines of this Italian gem, from secret waterfalls to magnificent views. Get your hiking boots on and lose yourself in the varied landscape around Lake Como.

1. Greenway del Lago:

Lakeside Stroll: is the first stop on the route. An attractive walking route that follows the perimeter of Lake Como is known as the Greenway del Lago. From Colonno to Griante, it's about 10 km long and has beautiful scenery along the lake, through quaint towns, and past old homes.

2. Parades del Viandante:

Trail of the Ancients: Along the eastern side of Lake Como winds the Sentiero del Viandante, also known as the Wayfarer's Path. Hikers may enjoy a scenic route through quaint villages and breathtaking vistas as they make their way from Colico to Lecco along this old track.

3. Monte Brunate:

Vista Elevation: Hike up to Monte Brunate for a beautiful panoramic view of Lake Como and the surrounding Alps. The path, beginning from Como, snakes through beautiful woodlands, presenting stunning panoramas at the peak.

4. Rifugio Menaggio to Monte Grona:

Alpine Challenge: For the adventurous hiker, the path from Rifugio Menaggio to Monte Grona provides a more strenuous climb. The reward at the peak provides vast views of Lake Como, the Grigna Range, and the Swiss Alps.

5. Path of the Wanderer (Sentiero del Wanderer):

Bellagio Beauty: This route, also known as the Sentiero del Wanderer, travels from Bellagio to the lovely town of Pescallo. Winding past cypress woods and olive orchards, it offers breathtaking views of the lake and adjacent hills.

6. Pigra – Colonno Trail:

Village Connection: The walk from Pigra to Colonno provides a picturesque route linking two attractive communities. Wander through chestnut trees and historic hamlets, immersing yourself in the calm of Lake Como's hinterland.

7. Villa del Balbianello a Lenno:

Garden Stroll: Begin your journey at the historic Villa del Balbianello and continue the route to Lenno. This lakeside route exposes hikers to sights of the villa's tiered gardens, picturesque towns, and the tranquil atmosphere of Lake Como.

8. Val Grande di Lanzo:

Nature Oasis: Val Grande di Lanzo is a wildlife reserve in Como, offering a calm escape for nature enthusiasts. Hike through lush woods, enjoy the calm of mountain streams, and explore the rich flora and wildlife of the area.

9. Waterfall of Acquafraggia:

Cascading Beauty: For a relaxing trek, enjoy the route to the Waterfall of Acquafraggia near Chiavenna. The route travels through forested regions and opens up to the breathtaking sight of the flowing waterfall—a fantastic site for a calm break.

10. Alpe di Nesso:

Mountain Village Charms: The Alpe di Nesso trek brings you to the lovely alpine town of Nesso. Wander through small lanes, observe stone buildings covered with flowers, and appreciate the calm of this hidden treasure.

Traveler's Tips:

Comfortable Footwear: Wear sturdy hiking boots to tackle rough terrain easily.

Water and Snacks: Carry ample water and food, particularly for longer walks, since some paths may not have suitable breaks.

Trail Maps: Obtain trail maps or utilize GPS navigation applications to guarantee you remain on the proper route.

Crafting Your Trail Symphony:

Lake Como's hiking and nature paths are not simply routes; they are compositions in nature's magnificent symphony. Whether you select a lakeside walk, an alpine climb, or a village-to-village tour, each step uncovers a new movement in this poetic trip. So, let the rustling leaves, magnificent panoramas, and hidden surprises become the notes in your hiking symphony along the beaches of Lake Como. Buon Cammino!

Museums and Historical Sites

Lake Como, a birthplace of history and culture, uncovers a treasure trove of museums and historical landmarks that relate stories of splendor, creativity, and the passage of time. From stately mansions to tiny museums, each location depicts the rich fabric of Lake Como's legacy. Step into the pages of history as we examine the cultural symphony that echoes through these outstanding monuments.

1. Villa Carlotta:

Botanical and Artistic Elegance: Villa Carlotta, hidden in Tremezzo, is a beautiful combination of art, architecture, and floral marvels. Explore beautiful sculptures, paintings, and a lush botanical garden including rare flora and blooming camellias.

2. Villa del Balbianello:

Lakeside Splendor: Villa del Balbianello, positioned on the western edge of Lake Como, is a tribute to elegance. This medieval estate features terraced gardens, Renaissance architecture, and beautiful views. It has acted as a film setting for renowned movies like "Casino Royale."

3. Como Cathedral (Cattedrale di Santa Maria Assunta):

Gothic Grandeur: The Como Cathedral, a marvel of Gothic architecture, dominates the city's skyline. Marvel at its elaborate exterior, beautiful stained glass windows, and the treasures inside, especially the Chapel of the Holy Nail.

4. Museo Didattico della Seta:

Silk Heritage: Located in Como, the Museo Didattico della Seta explores the region's silk industry. Discover the history of silk manufacturing, observe ancient weaving processes, and study the influence of this skill on the local economy.

5. Villa Serbelloni Gardens:

Botanical Enchantment: The grounds at Villa Serbelloni in Bellagio provide a lovely promenade among exotic plants, centuries-old trees, and vivid blossoms. Revel in the magnificent splendor that has captivated poets, authors, and painters for generations.

6. Museo Garibaldi:

Revolutionary Legacy: Museo Garibaldi in Como celebrates the heritage of Giuseppe Garibaldi, a crucial player in the Italian unification. The museum shows relics, papers, and memorabilia linked to Garibaldi's life and the Risorgimento.

7. Castello di Vezio:

Medieval Citadel: The Castello di Vezio, positioned above Varenna, is a medieval fortification with magnificent views of Lake Como. Explore its towers, dungeons, and beautiful environs while immersing yourself in the castle's ancient fascination.

8. Museo della Pesca:

Fishing Heritage: Located in Pianello del Lario, the Museo della Pesca (Fishing Museum) honors the region's fishing legacy. Discover traditional fishing gear, vessels, and the development of fishing activities on Lake Como.

9. Villa Monastero:

Scientific Retreat: Villa Monastero in Varenna is a medieval home turned scientific and cultural center. Wander through its floral garden, see the museum, and discover the old monastery that has sheltered intellectuals and scientists.

10. Museo Moto Guzzi:

Motorcycle Legacy: For aficionados of Italian engineering, the Museo Moto Guzzi in Mandello del Lario provides a riveting tour through the history of Moto Guzzi bikes. Admire antique models, learn about the brand's growth, and observe the passion behind these legendary machines.

Traveler's Tips:

Ticket Information: Check for ticket information and guided tour availability for historical sites and museums in advance.

Cultural Events: Inquire about any current cultural events, exhibits, or performances at these venues to improve your experience.

Photography Policies: Be careful of photographing rules, particularly in museums and ancient residences, to respect the cultural heritage.

Crafting Your Cultural Symphony:

Lake Como's museums and historical buildings are not ordinary structures; they are the magnificent chapters of a vast tale. Whether you meander through villa gardens, see ancient castles, or dig into silk manufacture, each encounter is a note in the rich cultural symphony that reverberates around the shores of Lake Como. So, let the creativity, history, and grace of these places become the lyrics in your study of this Italian masterpiece. Buona Esplorazione!

Events and Festivals

Lake Como, decorated with timeless beauty, provides a platform for a dynamic assortment of events and festivals throughout the year. From cultural events to musical extravaganzas, each gathering adds a new touch to the pleasant ambience of this Italian beauty. Join the celebrations as we explore the colorful schedule of activities that enliven the beaches of Lake Como.

1. Festival di Bellagio e del Lago di Como:

Cultural Soiree: The Festival di Bellagio e del Lago di Como is a cultural event hosted in Bellagio. Immerse yourself in art exhibits, classical music concerts, and dramatic productions that display the region's creative past.

2. Palio del Baradello:

Historical Joust: The Palio del Baradello, conducted in Como, is a medieval recreation involving a historical jousting contest. Witness knights in armor, colorful parades, and a bustling ambience reminiscent of medieval festivals.

3. Ferragosto Fireworks:

Midsummer Spectacle: Ferragosto, celebrated in mid-August, is distinguished by stunning fireworks displays around Lake Como. Join residents and tourists alike as the night sky glows with bursts of color, creating a magnificent mood.

4. Città di Como International Guitar Festival:

Musical Harmony: The Città di Como International Guitar Festival is a melodious festival hosted in Como, including famous guitarists from throughout the globe. Enjoy concerts, seminars, and workshops that resonate with the relaxing sounds of strings.

5. Sagra di San Giovanni:

Village Feast: The Sagra di San Giovanni is a traditional village feast conducted in Varenna on the feast day of St. John the Baptist. Delight in local food, music, and celebrations that reflect the atmosphere of this lakeside event.

6. Varenna Arte - Summer Concerts:

Lakeside Serenades: Varenna Arte conducts a series of summer performances that thrill lakeside crowds. From classical performances to modern melodies, these events enrich the summer nights with musical enchantment.

7. Como Film Festival:

Cinematic Showcase: The Como Film Festival offers cinematic splendor to the beaches of Lake Como. Enjoy screenings of indie and foreign films in unexpected venues, offering a cinematic experience that merges art and atmosphere.

8. Festival Tremezzina:

Artistic Spectrum: The Festival Tremezzina is a multidisciplinary festival including art, music, drama, and dance in several venues surrounding Lake Como. Immerse yourself in the many cultural manifestations that enliven the festival stages.

9. Notte Bianca Como:

White Night Extravaganza: Notte Bianca Como turns the city into a bustling center of activity. Experience a night of cultural activities, music, and entertainment that lasts till the early morning hours, creating a vibrant scene for residents and tourists alike.

10. Lake Como International Music Festival:

Global Harmony: The Lake Como International Music Festival welcomes performers from across the globe to play at enticing settings surrounding Lake Como. Revel in the richness of classical, jazz, and current music that echoes over the picturesque surroundings.

Traveler's Tips:

Event Schedules: Check event schedules and arrange your vacation to coincide with festivals or festivities that correspond with your interests.

Local Insights: Seek local suggestions for events and festivals to find hidden treasures that may not be generally recognised.

Cultural Participation: Embrace the local culture by participating in traditional events and connecting with the community during festivals.

Crafting Your Festive Overture:

Lake Como's events and festivals are not simply occasions; they are a celebration of culture, music, and the vivid spirit that animates this lovely area. Whether you are enthralled by fireworks, engrossed in cultural events, or savoring traditional feasts, let each event become a distinct note in your lakeside symphony. Buon Divertimento!

Chapter 7: Shopping in Lake Como

Local Markets

You are invited to stroll through the bustling local markets of Lake Como, a land of everlasting enchantment, where the rhythm of everyday life unfolds among fragrant fragrances and brilliant colors. Every market is a dynamic expression of the region's culture, offering fresh vegetables and handcrafted products. Come along as we tour the charming local markets that line the beaches of Lake Como, accompanied by lively harmonies.

1. Mercato di Bellagio

Lakeside Bazaar: Fresh food, local cheeses, handcrafted crafts, and more are plentiful at the Mercato di Bellagio, a lakeside market. Indulge in the vibrant ambiance while discovering the flavors and crafts that define Bellagio.

1. Mercato di Como:

A Touch of Urban Chic: Locals come to the Mercato di Como, a lively market in the middle of the city, to purchase meats, fresh produce, and regional delicacies. Like the city itself, the market is full of life and excitement.

3. Mercato di Lecco:

Waterside Bounty: Mercato di Lecco, nestled along the shores of Lake Como, provides a lovely combination of fresh fruit, handmade crafts, and local delights. Stroll among the kiosks and enjoy the gorgeous background of the lake.

4. Mercato di Menaggio:

Village Charms: Mercato di Menaggio, set in the picturesque town of Menaggio, offers a range of local items, from fruits and vegetables to handcrafted crafts. The market gives a peek into the laid-back lakeside lifestyle.

5. Mercato di Varenna:

Lakeside Elegance: Mercato di Varenna, facing Lake Como, is a lovely market where traders show an assortment of fresh fruit, flowers, and handcrafted goods. Enjoy the lakeside scenery as you browse the market's wares.

6. Mercato di Lenno:

Waterside Haven: Mercato di Lenno, on Lenno's shoreline, encourages tourists to taste the area's delicacies. From local cheeses and olives to handmade bread, the market embodies the spirit of Lenno's gastronomic tradition.

7. Mercato di Tremezzo:

Botanical Bliss: Mercato di Tremezzo is a beautiful market that emerges within Tremezzo's gorgeous surroundings. Engage with local merchants, experiencing the fragrances of fresh fruit, flowers, and other regional delicacies.

8. Mercato delle Valle Intelvi:

Mountain Marketplace: Mercato della Valle Intelvi, situated in the hilly area near Lake Como, exhibits a variety of local vegetables, cheeses, and handcrafted items. The market gives an insight into the culinary traditions of the neighboring regions.

9. Mercato di Colico:

Northern Charms: Mercato di Colico, located in the northern portion of Lake Como, provides a bustling market experience. Explore vendors providing local goods, homemade crafts, and a broad selection of gastronomic pleasures.

10. Mercato di Cernobbio:

Elegant Marketplace: Mercato di Cernobbio, in the town of Cernobbio, mixes metropolitan elegance with local market charm. Stroll around the booths, finding a mix of fresh food, handcrafted items, and regional delicacies.

Traveler's Tips:

Market Days: Check local calendars for market days in each town, since markets may be held on specified days of the week.

Cash Consideration: While some merchants may take cards, it's good to have cash, particularly in smaller markets.

Early Exploration: Visit markets in the morning to enjoy the bustling ambiance and get the finest variety of fresh items.

Crafting Your Market Sonata:

Lake Como's local markets are not only places to buy; they are a dynamic expression of the region's gastronomic diversity and artisanal innovation. Whether you're appreciating the perfume of fresh vegetables or finding handcrafted items, let each market visit become a distinct verse in your lakeside symphony. Buon Shopping!

Boutique Shops

Lake Como, a sanctuary of refinement, begs you to explore its variety of boutique shops—each a treasure trove of particular elegance. From high-end couture to handmade gifts, these businesses are the polished notes in the symphony of Lake Como's charm. Join the tour as we travel through the lovely streets, exploring the boutique jewels that grace the lakeside villages.

1. Carta Canta (Bellagio):

Artistic Stationery: Carta Canta in Bellagio is a store devoted to the art of stationery. Explore skillfully produced paper items, unusual writing implements, and stunning cards that reflect the spirit of the lakeside charm.

2. Chic and Cool (Como):

Fashion Oasis: trendy & Cool in Como is a store that curates a variety of trendy and modern apparel. Discover Italian and international designers, delivering a combination of refinement and current style.

3. Sartoria Rossi (Como):

Tailoring Excellence: Sartoria Rossi in Como typifies Italian tailoring brilliance. Step inside this store to experience handmade suits, fitted shirts, and beautiful accessories produced with painstaking attention to detail.

4. La Bottega di Brunella (Bellagio):

Linen Luxe: La Bottega di Brunella in Bellagio is a sanctuary for linen fans. Browse through a chosen assortment of handcrafted linen clothes, each item showcasing the unique workmanship typical with Lake Como.

5. Valentina (Varenna):

Artisanal Jewelry: Valentina in Varenna is a store that offers homemade jewelry inspired by the beauty of Lake Como. Adorn yourself with unique jewelry fashioned with precious stones and metals.

6. Pupa (Como):

Italian Footwear: Pupa in Como is a store specialised in Italian footwear. From trendy loafers to stunning heels, browse a chosen assortment of shoes that represent the classic Italian sense of design.

7. Pasticceria Poletti (Menaggio):

Sweet Temptations: Pasticceria Poletti in Menaggio is not simply a pastry store; it's a boutique of sweet pleasures. Indulge in handcrafted chocolates, pastries, and confections that are both scrumptious and attractively presented.

8. The Silk Museum Shop (Como):

Silk Splendors: The Silk Museum Shop in Como enables you to take a bit of the region's silk legacy home. Explore a range of silk scarves, accessories, and fabrics inspired by Como's rich silk legacy.

9. Nadia (Bellagio):

Bohemian Elegance: Nadia in Bellagio is a store that emanates boho elegance. Discover unusual apparel and accessories with a boho-chic flare, bringing a bit of free-spirited style to your lakeside wardrobe.

10. Gelateria Guidi (Lenno):

Gelato Delights: Gelateria Guidi in Lenno is not simply a gelateria; it's a shop of frozen treats. Indulge in gourmet gelato produced with local ingredients, creating a symphony of flavors that embody the spirit of Lake Como.

Traveler's Tips:

Local Artisans: Seek out businesses that sell things produced by local artists to enjoy the true beauty of Lake Como.

Custom Creations: Some shops may provide modification or customized services, enabling you to create a unique and personalized remembrance.

Hidden Gems: Explore the side streets and alleyways to unearth hidden boutique jewels that may not be as famous but provide unique treasures.

Crafting Your Boutique Sonata:

Lake Como's boutique stores are not merely places to shop; they are sanctuaries of elegance, workmanship, and sophisticated taste. Whether you're meandering along cobblestone lanes covered with elegant couture or finding handcrafted treasures, let each store visit become a different note in your lakeside symphony. Buon Shopping!

Souvenirs and Specialties

A veritable treasure trove of souvenirs and delicacies embodying Lake Como's enduring allure is available in this cultural haven and beauty haven. Every memento, from gastronomic pleasures to handcrafted crafts, adds a harmonious accent to the tapestry of your moments spent by the lake. Come with us as we delve into the magical realm of Lake Como mementoes and specialities.

1 .Olive Oil from Lake Como:

Liquid Gold: Pick yourself a bottle of Lake Como olive oil made right here in the region. A culinary treasure that reflects the region's long agricultural history, Como olive oil is renowned for its delicate flavor and excellent quality.

2. Como Silk Accents:

Stylish Threads: Use scarves and ties made of Como silk to envelop yourself in opulence. These items are the perfect mementoes of the region's silk craftsmanship—timeless and exquisitely designed with a smooth touch.

3. Lariano Honey:

Nature's Sweetness: Lariano honey, produced in the Lake Como region, is a wonderful delicacy. The honey represents the rich flora of the area and is a pleasant reminder of the natural splendor that surrounds Lake Como.

4. Como Artisanal Pasta:

Flavors of Tradition: Bring home a taste of Como with handcrafted pasta. Crafted with care and frequently fashioned in ancient ways, Como's pasta lets you taste the unique flavors of the area in your own home.

5. Lakeside Ceramics:

Art in Clay: Explore local ceramics created by talented artists. From ornamental pieces to useful dinnerware, Como's ceramics are a tribute to the region's creative legacy and make for distinctive and attractive keepsakes.

6. Lake Como Limoncello:

Citrus Symphony: Limoncello is a popular local delicacy blended with the vivid tastes of lemons from Lake Como. Bring home a bottle of this citrus liqueur to taste the zesty spirit of the area.

7. Como Lakefront Art Prints:

Scenic Impressions: Purchase art prints highlighting the stunning scenery of Lake Como. These prints capture the lyrical beauty of the area and serve as visual keepsakes of your lakeside trip.

8. Lavender Products from Vezio:

Aromatherapy Bliss: Vezio, noted for its lavender fields, provides a selection of lavender-infused items. From sachets to essential oils, these goods bring the relaxing aroma of Lake Como's lavender into your everyday life.

9. Bellagio Handcrafted Jewelry:

Wearable Art: Bellagio is known for its exquisite jewels. Explore local stores for unique goods that exhibit the workmanship and design inspired by the beauty of Lake Como.

10. Como Lakeside Coffee Blends:

Aromatic Awakening: Indulge in the rich tastes of Como's coffee blends. Specially developed to represent the region's coffee culture, these blends provide a sense of the fragrant enchantment that pervades Lake Como's cafés.

Traveler's Tips:

Local Markets: Explore local markets for a broad assortment of souvenirs and specialities, sometimes offered by craftsmen and producers.

Authenticity: Look for goods that feature the "Made in Lake Como" or "Made in Italy" logo to assure authenticity and support local craftsmen.

packing: Consider the packing of your mementoes, since many goods come in nicely designed boxes or bags that contribute to their visual appeal.

Crafting Your Lakeside Memoir:

Lake Como's souvenirs and specialities are not simply symbols; they represent a tangible link to the region's spirit. Whether you're sampling local tastes, beautifying yourself with handcrafted treasures, or bringing the atmosphere of Lake Como into your home, let each memento become a treasured note in the song of your lakeside memories. Buon Ricordo!

Chapter 8: Day Trips and Excursions

Nearby Attractions

While Lake Como's beauty is compelling, the surrounding area uncovers a tapestry of attractions that offer dimension to your lakeside experience. You may add a new song to the exploring symphony at every neighboring treasure, from historic towns to picturesque getaways. Come us as we explore the picturesque areas around Lake Como, going beyond its shoreline to uncover hidden gems.

1. Villa Olmo (Como):

 Neo-Classical splendor: Discover the opulence of the neoclassical Villa Olmo in Como, set amid verdant grounds. Explore the old estate's terraced park, take in the breathtaking views of Lake Como, and marvel at the elegant architecture.

2. Swiss Border Towns (Chiasso and Lugano)

Border Crossing: Chiasso and Lugano are two charming Swiss cities that are easily accessible by car from Lake Como. In this picturesque Swiss town, you can taste authentic Swiss food, stroll through quaint alleys, and learn about the rich cultural history that combines Italian and Swiss influences.

3. Isola Comacina:

Island Retreat: Take a boat ride to Isola Comacina, a lovely island in Lake Como. Explore the relics of old churches, eat in waterfront restaurants, and enjoy the calm of this tiny but historically rich island.

4. Bellano Ravine and Orrido di Bellano:

Nature's Gorge: Discover the Bellano Ravine and Orrido di Bellano, a natural canyon cut by the Pioverna River. Walk along suspended walkways and watch the force of nature as the river rushes through this beautiful geological creation.

5. Villa Balbianello Gardens (Lenno):

Botanical Bliss: While Villa Balbianello is a well-known sight, don't miss admiring its lovely gardens near Lenno. Wander through terraced landscapes filled with bright flowers, cypress trees, and sculptures overlooking Lake Como.

6. Cernobbio Waterfront:

Lakeside Charm: Explore the lovely waterfront of Cernobbio, famed for its exquisite residences, cafés, and gorgeous promenade. Admire the architecture, enjoy lakefront eating, and relax in the tranquil environment of this lakeside town.

7. Como-Brunate Funicular:

Panoramic Ascent: Take the Como-Brunate funicular for a picturesque excursion to the mountain village of Brunate. Enjoy stunning panoramic views of Lake Como and the surrounding Alps from this unique vantage point.

8. San Martino Church (Bellagio):

Spiritual Splendor: Visit the San Martino Church in Bellagio, an architectural marvel with a history extending back to the 12th century. Marvel at its frescoes, sculptures, and calm environment that takes you to another age.

9. Villa d'Este Gardens (Cernobbio):

Renaissance Elegance: Explore the grounds of Palace d'Este in Cernobbio, a Renaissance palace surrounded by tiered landscapes and fountains. Wander along the complex paths, appreciating the beautiful combination of art and nature.

10. Monte Grona (Pigra):

Mountain Panorama: For trekking lovers, climb Monte Grona near Pigra for panoramic views of Lake Como, the surrounding mountains, and the Swiss Alps. The arduous trek is rewarded with spectacular scenery.

Traveler's Tips:

Local Transportation: Utilize local transit alternatives, like ferries and funiculars, for a picturesque and quick way to visit neighbouring sights.

Seasonal Considerations: Some sites may have seasonal opening hours, so check in advance, particularly if you intend to visit at specified seasons of the year.

Guided Tours: Consider attending guided tours to acquire insights into the history, culture, and natural beauty of neighboring destinations.

Crafting Your Lakeside Expedition:

Lake Como's neighboring sites are not simply pauses; they are intriguing chapters that enhance the vast tale of your lakeside vacation. Whether you're discovering ancient homes, enjoying panoramic landscapes, or diving into nature's treasures, let each surrounding site become a harmonizing note in the symphony of your Lake Como tour. Buon Viaggio!

Guided Tours

Embark on a customized trip across Lake Como's beauty and history with guided excursions that expose the region's secrets and tales. Let skilled guides accompany you around the gorgeous landscapes, ancient homes, and cultural riches, complementing your lakeside experience with fascinating storytelling. Join the excursion as we dig into the fascination of guided trips around Lake Como.

1. Villa del Balbianello Tour:

Architectural Tale: Explore the magnificent home del Balbianello with a guided tour that uncovers the architectural wonders, lush gardens, and cinematic history of this legendary home. Gain insights into this villa's background and its significance in numerous films.

2. Como City Walking Tour:

Urban Elegance: Immerse yourself in the beauty of Como's old town with a guided walking tour. Stroll through old streets, see prominent buildings like the Como Cathedral, and experience the city's cultural and architectural riches.

3. Bellagio Village Discovery:

Lakeside Charms: Discover the lovely hamlet of Bellagio with a guided tour that navigates its cobblestone alleys, lakeside promenades, and ancient landmarks. Learn about the village's cultural past and its importance on the shores of Lake Como.

4. Varenna Highlights Tour:

Picturesque Exploration: Join a guided tour of Varenna to experience its gorgeous promenades, ancient landmarks, and quaint lanes. Gain insights into the local culture, explore attractions like Villa Monastero, and experience the serene environment of this lakeside jewel.

5. Isola Comacina Boat Tour:

Island Odyssey: Embark on a boat journey to Isola Comacina with a skilled guide. Learn about the island's history, tour old churches and archaeological sites, and appreciate the tranquil beauty of this unique place.

6. Como-Brunate Funicular Tour:

Panoramic Ascent: Experience the Como-Brunate funicular with a guided trip that takes you on a picturesque ride to Brunate. Enjoy breathtaking views of Lake Como, learn about the history of the funicular, and explore the hillside town.

7. Silk Heritage Walk in Como:

Threads of Tradition: Delve into the silk tradition of Como with a guided tour that examines the city's silk-related landmarks. Visit the Silk Museum, understand the history of silk manufacture, and admire the workmanship behind Como's silk culture.

8. Villa Carlotta Garden Tour:

Botanical Wonders: Take a guided tour of Villa Carlotta's magnificent gardens in Tremezzo. Explore the botanical variety, learn about rare plant species, and admire the artistic and natural components that make this home a horticultural wonder.

9. Lake Como Food and Wine Tour:

Culinary Symphony: Indulge in the tastes of Lake Como with a guided food and wine tour. Visit local markets, sample regional delicacies, and savor carefully matched wines, immersing yourself in the gastronomic joys of the area.

10. Como Lakefront Art Exploration:

Cultural Soiree: Join a guided trip that explores the Lake Como lakefront's artistic gems. Visit galleries, see public art projects, and acquire insights into the cultural relevance of art along the shores of Lake Como.

Traveler's Tips:

Booking in Advance: Reserve guided tours in advance, particularly for popular destinations, to reserve your position and assure availability.

Multilingual Guides: Look for tours with bilingual guides to boost your knowledge and appreciation of the tales given throughout the journey.

trained excursions: Consider specialist excursions, such as photography tours or historical-themed walks, to personalize the experience to your interests.

Crafting Your Guided Odyssey:

Lake Como's guided excursions are not simply travels; they are tailored odysseys that unravel the region's rich fabric. Whether you're touring ancient homes, walking through picturesque towns, or enjoying gastronomic pleasures, let each guided tour be a riveting chapter in the immersive tale of Lake Como. Buon Viaggio!

Scenic Drives

Embark on a trip of spectacular beauty as you cross the picturesque roadways that encircle the shores of Lake Como. These meandering roads disclose breathtaking views, beautiful settlements, and the ageless fascination of the surrounding surroundings. Join the excursion as we travel the lovely roads that create a magnificent painting surrounding Lake Como.

1. SS340 - The Western Shore Drive:

Lakeside Elegance: Embark on the SS340 for a beautiful trip around Lake Como's western side. Meander through picturesque communities like Lenno and Tremezzo, with vistas of magnificent houses and the clean seas as your constant companions.

2. SP44 - Bellagio Peninsula Drive:

Bellagio Beauty: Explore the Bellagio Peninsula by following the SP44, a picturesque road that encircles this wonderful location. Enjoy magnificent vistas of the lake, cypress-lined lanes, and glimpses of Bellagio's beauty at every turn.

3. SS583 - Como to Lecco Lakeside Drive:

Riviera di Lecco Delights: Travel along the SS583 from Como to Lecco for a lakeside adventure that showcases the Riviera di Lecco's natural splendor. Admire the mountains, lovely villages, and the serene atmosphere of Lake Como.

4. SS36 - Lake Como Eastern Shore Drive:

Majestic Landscapes: Take the SS36 for a trip along Lake Como's eastern side, affording breathtaking views of the lake and the surrounding Alps. Pass through communities like Colico and Mandello del Lario, relishing the various sceneries.

5. Via Regina - Historic Lakeside Route:

Historical Pathway: Follow the Via Regina, an old Roman route, for a historic lakeside trip. This journey takes you past scenic towns, like Moltrasio and Laglio, with views of medieval architecture and lakeside beauty.

6. SP27 - Intelvi Valley Adventure:

Mountain Majesty: Head into the Intelvi Valley via the SP27 for a rugged adventure. This gorgeous route unfolds through verdant valleys, and lovely hamlets, and gives magnificent perspectives of Lake Como and the neighboring Alps.

7. SS340 - Central Lake Road:

Central Charms: Cruise along the SS340 across the centre portion of Lake Como, going via Menaggio and Bellano. Enjoy views of the lake, distant mountains, and the ever-changing panorama that marks the heart of Lake Como.

8. SS583 - Lakeside Drive to Bellano:

Waterfront Serenity: Take the SS583 for a lovely lakeside drive heading to Bellano. Revel in the calm of the lake, beautiful sceneries, and the pleasant atmosphere of Bellano's shoreline.

9. SP41 - Argegno to Menaggio Drive:

Village Vistas: Navigate the SP41 from Argegno to Menaggio for a journey that uncovers lovely towns and spectacular lake vistas. Admire the countryside as you travel through small hamlets, each with its distinct character.

10. SS340 - Como to Cernobbio Riviera Drive:

Riviera Splendors: Drive along the SS340 from Como to Cernobbio for a drive along the Riviera that highlights the magnificence of Lake Como. Enjoy vistas of stately houses, beautiful gardens, and the timeless beauty of the lakefront.

Traveler's Tips:

picturesque pauses: Plan pauses at picturesque vistas or lakeside villages to truly experience the scenery along the trip.

Off-Peak Exploration: Consider exploring these routes at off-peak hours to enjoy calmer roads and a more relaxed driving experience.

Photography Essentials: Bring a camera to capture the amazing scenery and sights along the drives.

Crafting Your Scenic Symphony:

Lake Como's picturesque drives are not merely roads; they are lyrical symphonies that expose the region's natural grandeur. Whether you're tracking the coastline or climbing steep routes, let each gorgeous journey become a hypnotic piece in the symphony of your Lake Como adventure. Buon Viaggio!

Chapter 9: Practical Tips

Money Matters

Embarking on your Lake Como excursion includes not only relishing the scenery but also handling money problems with care. Here's a financial preparation to guarantee your lakeside stay is as smooth as the lovely waves of Lake Como.

1. Currency and Payment Methods:

Euro Excellence: Italy utilizes the Euro (€), so ensure you have local cash for minor purchases. Major credit cards are frequently accepted, but it's essential to carry extra cash, particularly in smaller towns or markets.

2. ATMs and Banks:

Strategic Withdrawals: ATMs are frequently accessible in locations near Lake Como. Opt for bank ATMs for safe transactions. Notify your bank of your trip dates to avoid any complications with card use overseas.

3. Currency Exchange:

Strategic Exchanges: While major towns provide currency exchange facilities, the prices may vary. Consider exchanging a little amount at the airport or your native country for early expenditures and convenience.

4. Tipping Etiquette:

Gratitude Gesture: Tipping is typical at restaurants and for services. Round up the amount or give a 10% to 15% tip. It's not essential, but a sign of thanks is encouraged.

5. Budgeting for Activities:

Lakeside Leisure: Plan your budget considering the activities you desire to partake in. Whether it's visiting villas, taking guided excursions, or eating local food, budget cash properly.

6. Accommodation Costs:

Lakeside Lodgings: Accommodation fees vary, and Lake Como provides alternatives from boutique hotels to beautiful guesthouses. Research and book in advance to ensure good prices, particularly during high seasons.

7. Dining Expenses:

Culinary Delights: Dining expenditures might vary, with lakefront restaurants frequently having higher charges. Explore local trattorias for genuine experiences and consider integrating some self-catering alternatives for a budget-friendly balance.

8. Transportation Costs:

Scenic Commutes: Plan for transportation expenditures, including boat excursions, ferry voyages, or funicular travels. Consider transit passes or cards for convenience and possibly savings on numerous journeys.

9. Shopping Considerations:

Boutique Splurges: Factor in shopping fees for souvenirs, boutique discoveries, or local specialties. Set a budget for indulgences and explore local markets for unique, budget-friendly discoveries.

10. Emergency Preparedness:

Financial Safeguards: Carry a credit card for emergencies, and be aware of the contact details for your bank or credit card provider in case of any complications. Keep a photocopy of crucial papers like passports and credit cards.

Traveler's Tips:

Local SIM Card: Consider buying a local SIM card for your phone to avoid international roaming costs and have access to local services and data.

Dynamic Exchange Rates: Monitor exchange rates and consider utilizing currency conversion applications for real-time information on the move.

Language and Numbers: Learn a few basic Italian words for transactions, and acquaint yourself with numbers to improve communication during purchases.

Crafting Your Financial Sonata:

Lake Como's attractiveness is not simply visual; it's a sensual experience that involves the prudent management of financial problems. As you explore the sceneries and revel in lakeside pleasures, let your financial preparations become the harmonic background to the symphony of your Lake Como stay. Buon Viaggio!

Language Basics

Immerse yourself in the melodic cadence of Italian as you walk into the magnificent region of Lake Como. While many people speak English, adopting a few Italian words adds a harmonic touch to your lakeside trip. Let's study some language fundamentals to better your connection with the culture and people of Lake Como.

1. Greetings and Politeness:

Buongiorno (Buongiorno): Good morning
Buonasera (Bwon-a-se-ra): Good evening
Grazie (Gra-tsyeh): Thank you

Per favore (Per favore): Please
Prego (Pre-go): You're welcome

2. Common Phrases:

Ciao (Chow): Hello/Goodbye (Informal)
Come stai? (Come stai): How are you?
Mi chiamo... (Mee kyah-mo): My name is...
Mi dispiace (Mee dee-spya-che): I'm sorry
Posso avere il conto? (Po-so a-ver-re il con-to): Can I get the bill?

3. Getting Around:

Dove si trova...? (Dove si trova): Where is...?
Stazione (Stazione): Train station
Bagno (Ban-yo): Bathroom
Biglietto (Big-lyet-to): Ticket

4. Numbers:

Uno (Oo-no): One
Due (Doo-e): Two
Tre (Tre): Three
Dieci (Die-chi): Ten

5. Dining Etiquette:

Menu, per favore (Me-nu, per fa-vo-re): Menu, please
Acqua (Ak-kwa): Water
Vino (Vee-no): Wine
Primo piatto (Pree-mo pyar-to): First course
Il conto, per favore (Il conto, per fa-vo-re): The bill, please

6. Navigating Transportation:

Autobus (Au-to-bus): Bus
Stazione ferroviaria (Stazione ferroviaria): Train station
Fermata (Fer-ma-ta): Bus stop
Destinazione (Des-ti-na-zlo-ne): Destination

7. Shopping Phrases:

Quanto costa? (Kwan-to kos-ta): How much does it cost?
Posso pagare con carta di credito? (Posso pagare con carta di credito): Can I pay with a credit card?
Sconto (Skon-to): Discount
Negozio (Negozio): Shop

8. Emergencies:

Aiuto (Ai-u-to): Help
Polizia (Po-lit-zi-a): Police
Ospedale (Os-pe-da-le): Hospital
Numero di emergenza (Num-ero di emergenza): Emergency number

9. Expressing Appreciation:

Bellissimo (Bel-lis-si-mo): Beautiful
Delizioso (De-li-zio-so): Delicious
Magnifico (Mag-ni-fi-co): Magnificent
Grazie mille (Gra-Hsieh mil-le): Thank you very lot

10. Local Courtesy:

Rispetto per la cultura locale (Rispetto per la cultura lo-ca-le): Respect for local culture
Sorridi (Sor-ri-di): Smile
Assapora ogni momento (As-sa-po-ra og-ni mo-men-to): Savor every moment
Conversazione leggera (Con-ver-sa-zio-ne leggera): Light chat

Traveler's Tips:

Language Apps: Consider language learning apps for fast and handy sessions on the move.
Friendly Gestures: Italians are expressive, so don't hesitate to utilise gestures to communicate meaning.

Local Pronunciations: Pay attention to local pronunciations to increase communication and be well-received.

Crafting Your Linguistic Aria:

Lake Como's splendor is complemented by the poetic appeal of the Italian language. As you visit its coasts, let these linguistic essentials become the lyrical notes that resonate with the culture, people, and soul-stirring vistas of this Italian treasure. Buon Viaggio!

Safety and Health Tips

As you begin on the wonderful voyage around Lake Como, safeguarding your safety and well-being is a major tune in the symphony of your vacation experience. Let's compile a thorough score of safety and health suggestions to choreograph a harmonic and worry-free trip.

1. Travel Insurance Overture:

Melodic Protection: Begin your adventure with the overture of travel insurance. Ensure it covers medical crises, trip cancellations, and other unexpected situations, establishing a harmonic safety net for your trips.

2. Health Prelude:

Immunization Sonata: Check whether any immunisations are recommended before flying to Italy. Common immunisations include Hepatitis A and B, influenza, and regular injections.

3. Sun Protection Interlude:

Radiant Defense: The lakeside sun may be welcoming yet strong. Include sunscreen, sunglasses, and a hat with your wardrobe to defend yourself from the sun's rays.

4. Water Sonata:

Hydration Harmony: Stay hydrated with bottled or tap water, which is typically safe to drink in Lake Como. Carry a reusable water bottle to drink on the move and maintain a good hydration cadence.

5. Footwear Cadence:

Comfortable Stride: The lakefront landscape may feature cobblestone pathways and rough walks. Opt for comfortable, durable shoes to traverse the lovely towns and experience the stunning scenery with ease.

6. Mosquito Defense Crescendo:

Repellent Rhapsody: Embrace the lovely nights near the lake but be prepared for mosquitos. Pack bug repellant to guarantee a restful night's sleep without any annoying buzzing.

7. Dining Harmony:

Culinary Cadence: Savor the local food with confidence. Check food hygiene ratings, luxuriate in well-cooked meals, and consider dietary limitations to create a symphony of pleasurable eating experiences.

8. Transportation Ballad:

Safe Sojourns: Whether boating the lake or roaming through cities, consider safety in transportation. Follow local restrictions, find reliable services, and experience the musical cadence of calm journeys.

9. Emergency Nocturne:

Knowledgeable Refrain: Familiarize oneself with emergency numbers and the location of medical institutions. A well-prepared traveller can promptly negotiate any unanticipated medical or safety notes.

10. Weather Harmonics:

Forecast Finale: Lake Como's weather may be different. Check predictions and pack appropriately. From light layers for cold nights to sun protection for sunny days, let your wardrobe dance with the weather's varied rhythms.

Traveler's Tips:

Pharmacy Familiarity: Identify the locations of pharmacies in the places you'll be visiting for any over-the-counter requirements or minor health issues.

Local Health Services: Be aware of the nearby hospitals or clinics. Many communities have medical facilities with English-speaking personnel.

Allergy Awareness: If you have allergies or special health issues, pack appropriate medicines and warn travel companions or tour guides.

Crafting Your Safety and Health Opus:

Lake Como's magnificence is best experienced when your well-being is in perfect balance. As you explore its coastlines, let this safety and health advice create a musical soundtrack, ensuring your voyage is not only visually attractive but also a symphony of safety, health, and calm discovery. Buon Viaggio!

Useful Contacts

A well-orchestrated trip experience around Lake Como requires possessing a repertory of beneficial connections. From local help to emergency services, let's establish a symphony of connections to guarantee your travel is accompanied by a harmonic support network.

1. Emergency Services Crescendo:

Emergency Number (Italy): 112
Medical Emergency (118): For emergency medical help, contact 118.

2. Local Authorities Overture:

Local Police (Carabinieri): 112 or 113
Local Police (Polizia Locale): Numbers vary by town; ask locally.

3. Medical Assistance Harmony:

Hospital (Ospedale): Identify the closest hospital; Como's major hospital is Ospedale Sant'Anna.
Pharmacy (Farmacia): Local pharmacies give over-the-counter drugs and health advice.

4. Transportation Symphony:

Ferry Information: Contact local ferry firms for timetables and routes.
Public Transportation: Inquire about local bus or rail services for transportation questions.

5. Tourist Information Rhapsody:

Lake Como Tourism Office: Obtain tourist information and help.
Local Tour Operators: Contact suggested tour operators for guided excursions.

6. Embassy and Consulate Sonata:

Embassy/Consulate Contacts: Know the contact information for your country's embassy or consulate in Italy for help.

7. Accommodation Cadence:

Accommodation Front Desk: Keep your accommodation's front desk or reception number accessible for any queries.

8. Language Assistance Interlude:

Language Translation Apps: Download language translation applications for instant communication aid.

9. Local Guides and Tours Duet:

Guided Tours: Save contact information for any guided tours or local guides you interact with.

10. Travel Insurance Refrain:

Travel Insurance Provider: Keep your travel insurance provider's contact information for help.

Traveler's Tips:

Saved Contacts: Save critical contacts on your phone and preserve a printed list as a backup.

Local SIM Card: Consider buying a local SIM card for your phone for easier contact with local services.

Language Assistance applications: Download applications that aid with language translation and communication.

Crafting Your Contact Sonata:

Lake Como's attractiveness is enhanced when you have a harmonious network of beneficial relationships. As you tour the stunning landscapes and lovely cities, let these vital tunes accompany your trip, assuring a symphony of support, information, and help. Buon Viaggio!

Chapter 10: Photography Guide

Best Photo Spots

Set off on a photography adventure around Lake Como, where the picturesque scenery, classic buildings, and irresistible Italian charm are captured in every shot. Each of these top picture places adds its special touch to the visual symphony that is Lake Como, therefore we've put them here for your perusal.

1. Villa del Balbianello (Lenno):

lakefront mansion: Nestled on the western beach, Villa del Balbianello captures the timeless beauty. The tiered gardens of the house, with their sculptures and cypress trees, provide a lovely setting against the reflective lake.

2. Bellagio Promenade:

Appeal of Cobblestones: Take in the sights and sounds of lakeside living as you stroll down Bellagio's picturesque promenade. A picture-perfect arrangement is achieved by the multi-coloured structures, cafés by the lake, and the view of the neighboring mountains.

1. Varenna's strong suits:

Village Panorama: Climb up to Castello di Vezio or visit the floral gardens of Villa Monastero in Varenna for panoramic views of the hamlet, Lake Como, and the distant Alps.

4. Como Cathedral Square:

Architectural Elegance: The Como Cathedral and its plaza are an architectural feast for your lens. Capture the exquisite features of the church against the background of the busy plaza.

5. Brunate Funicular Viewpoint:

Panoramic Heights: Take the funicular to Brunate for a higher view. The panoramic views of Lake Como, the town, and the surrounding hills make a stunning scenario for your camera.

6. Isola Comacina:

Island Serenity: Capture the calm of Isola Comacina from a boat or one of the lakeside overlooks. The island's antique ruins and scenic backdrop combine for a timeless shot.

7. Maggie's Waterfront:

Lakeside Charm: Wander around Menaggio's shoreline absorbing the splendor of colorful houses, lakeside promenades, and the breathtaking vista across the lake.

8. Tremezzo's Villa Carlotta Gardens:

Botanical Beauty: Explore the lovely grounds of Villa Carlotta in Tremezzo. Photograph colorful flowers, old trees, and the creative intricacies of this floral wonderland.

9. Sunset at Colico:

Golden Hour Glow: Head to Colico's lakefront after sunset, capturing the golden colours reflected on the water and shadows of the neighboring mountains.

10. Scenic Drives and Viewpoints:

SS340 and Beyond: Embrace the splendor along beautiful highways like SS340, catching perspectives in Lenno, Bellagio, and other places. Each turn uncovers a fresh visual wonder.

Traveler's Tips:

Golden Hour Magic: Plan your photographic outings between the golden hours of dawn and sunset for spectacular lighting.

Weather Adaptability: Be adaptable with your ideas dependent on weather conditions to capture the diverse moods of Lake Como.

Boat and Ferry Perspectives: Consider taking a boat or ferry for unusual viewpoints of lakeside villages and villas from the water.

Crafting Your Visual Symphony:

Lake Como's appeal is visually captivating, and each shot site lends a melodious note to the visual symphony. As you frame your photographs, let the beauty of the lake, attractive villages, and architectural treasures merge into a timeless photographic composition. Buon Viaggio!

Capture the Essence of Lake Como

Lake Como, a lyrical beauty, compels photographers to catch its essence—where turquoise waters meet green hills, and old palaces whisper stories of grandeur. Embark on a visual trip, framed by the stunning scenery, quaint villages, and cultural treasures that constitute the spirit of Lake Como.

1. Morning Serenity:

Dawn's Embrace: Capture the serene sunrise as mist dances across the lake, shrouding the villas in an ethereal hue. Morning fisherman, distant church bells, and the calm lapping of water make a tranquil lakeside sonnet.

2. Lakeside Villas:

Architectural Poetry: Frame the gorgeous homes along the shore—Villa del Balbianello's tiered gardens, Villa Carlotta's floral symphony, and the ageless charm of Villa Balbiano. Each conveys a narrative of richness and history.

3. Bellagio's Ambiance:

Piazza Melody: Capture the bustling vibe of Bellagio's Piazza della Chiesa. Vibrant cafés, cobblestone streets, and the vista of the lake's three branches weave together in a true Italian tapestry.

4. Varenna's Charms:

Village Elegance: Stroll through Varenna's streets, catching the splendor of colorful buildings, lakeside cafés, and the ancient grandeur of Castello di Vezio. Each nook vibrates with the village's ageless elegance.

5. Como's Urban Symphony:

Cathedral Grandeur: Frame the Como Cathedral against the urban symphony of Piazza del Duomo. The cathedral's Gothic beauty is a tribute to Como's rich cultural legacy.

6. Lakeside Funicular Views:

Brunate's Panorama: Ascend to Brunate via the funicular for panoramic sights. Capture Lake Como's expanse, the town below, and the distant Alps—a visual crescendo of nature's majesty.

7. Island Tranquility:

Isola Comacina's Silence: Photograph the tranquil beauty of Isola Comacina. Ancient ruins, rich flora, and the island's isolated atmosphere create a visual sonnet of peace.

8. Charming Menaggio:

Waterfront Symphony: Wander around Menaggio's shoreline absorbing the vitality of lakeside life. Boat reflections, lakeside promenades, and the distant hills make a wonderful lakeside song.

9. Tremezzo's Botanical Harmony:

Villa Carlotta's Rhapsody: Explore the floral harmony of Villa Carlotta's gardens. Enchanting blossoms, sculptures, and the reflection of the house in the water form a magnificent ballet of nature and art.

10. Sunset Sonata:

Golden Hour Finale: Conclude your visual voyage with the golden colors of sunset. Capture the sun saying adieu, pouring warmly on the lake, and changing the surroundings into a magnificent painting.

Traveler's Tips:

Local Faces and Stories: Capture impromptu images of locals and their experiences to give a human aspect to your visual story.

Weather's Emotional Palette: Embrace the ever-changing weather to capture varied moods—from foggy mornings to spectacular storms, each exhibiting a part of Lake Como's character.

Reflections and Water Play: Utilize the lake's reflecting surface for interesting pictures, emphasizing symmetry and the interaction of light.

Crafting Your Visual Opus:
Lake Como's essence is an endless inspiration for photographers, urging them to build a visual masterwork. As you frame each image, let the spirit of the lake—the peacefulness, architectural beauty, and cultural richness—become the notes in your everlasting photographic symphony. Buon Viaggio!

Chapter 11: Conclusion

Final Thoughts and Recommendations

As your vacation around Lake Como concludes, let the echoes of its enchantment remain, producing a symphony of memories that resound with eternal beauty, rich culture, and tranquil surroundings. Here are some concluding ideas and tips to capture your Lake Como trip.

1. Reflective Moments:

Pause and Absorb: Find a calm lakeside area to reflect on your travels. Let the peacefulness of the river and the surrounding sceneries imprint lasting memories.

2. Culinary Memoirs:

Savor the Flavors: Relish a last Italian feast, trying local delights. Whether it's a lakefront trattoria or a hidden treasure in the alleyways, let the aromas of Lake Como linger on your palette.

3. Lingering Lakeside Strolls:

Stroll and Absorb: Take a leisurely lakeside walk, savouring the architectural splendor, the glistening waterways, and the beautiful marriage of nature and human artistry.

4. Sunset Farewell:

Sunset Send-off: Bid adieu to Lake Como with a sunset goodbye. Find a panoramic perspective, see the sun's golden embrace, and let the colours of twilight etch a lyrical memories.

5. Expressive Photography:

Visual Chronicle: Review your photographic chronicle. Each photograph depicts a chapter of your Lake Como story—villas, cobblestone streets, and the delicate emotions of this Italian beauty.

6. Local Artisanal Souvenirs:

Artistic Mementos: Explore local marketplaces for handcrafted items. Choose items that represent the region's workmanship, giving a touch of Lake Como to your life back home.

7. Friendly Connections:

Cultural Conversations: Cherish the ties built with locals and other travelers. Exchange tales, humor, and possibly contact information, building cultural relationships.

8. Gratitude for the Journey:

Heartfelt Thank You: Express thankfulness for the trip. Whether via a diary entry, a passionate email, or a simple moment of gratitude, celebrate the enchantment of Lake Como.

9. Future Serenades:

Dreams of Return: As you wave arrivederci to Lake Como, leave a place in your heart for future serenades. The lake's appeal guarantees that the symphony of its beauty remains an eternal invitation.

10. Buon Viaggio Farewell:

Wishing Well: In the spirit of "Buon Viaggio" (Safe Travels), bring the essence of Lake Como with you. May your future adventures be graced with the same feeling of surprise, discovery, and quiet beauty.

Traveler's Tips:

Travel notebook: Record your thoughts, emotions, and unforgettable events in a travel notebook to recall the intricacies of your Lake Como journey.

Connect Digitally: Stay connected with newfound friends and share your Lake Como memories via digital channels, establishing a permanent network of shared experiences.

Plan the Encore: Consider arranging a return to Lake Como to explore new areas, find hidden beauties, and let the lake's enchantment grab you once again.

Closing Notes:

Lake Como is not simply a destination; it's a symphony of experiences that connects with the spirit. As you wave goodbye to its beaches, may the echoes of its beauty follow you on your future trips, acting as a reminder of the wonder that lies in every corner of the earth. Buon Viaggio!

Chapter 12: Appendix

Maps and Diagrams

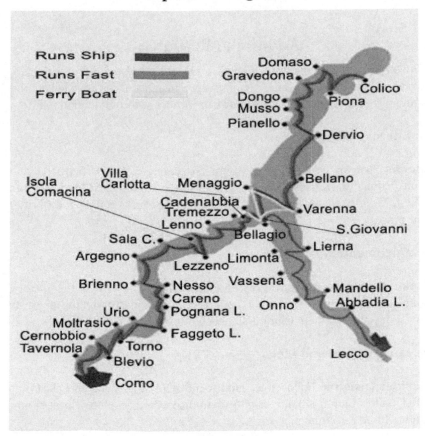

Maps and schematics of Lake Como serve as visual gates, revealing the geographical symphony of attractive villages, antique villas, and magnificent landscapes. From the complex pattern of cobblestone alleys in Bellagio to the grandeur of villas along the seashore, these visual aids offer a vivid image, taking guests through the eternal beauty and cultural tapestry of this Italian masterpiece. Whether planning an itinerary or reminiscing about the voyage, these maps and diagrams reflect the spirit of Lake Como's charm.

Additional Resources

As you journey into the lovely environment of Lake Como, a treasure trove of extra information awaits, giving deeper insights, local knowledge, and immersive experiences. Elevate your trip with these recommendations:

1. Literary Escapades:

Books Set in Lake Como: Immerse yourself in the fictitious and non-fictional narratives set against the background of Lake Como. Authors like E.M. Forster, Alessandro Manzoni, and Tim Parks convey the spirit of the place.

2. Documentary Discoveries:

Lake Como Documentaries: Explore films that reveal the history, culture, and natural beauty of Lake Como. Visual storytelling gives an engaging companion to your on-site encounters.

3. Local Guides and Blogs:

Insider Insights: Follow local guides and read blogs made by Lake Como aficionados. Gain firsthand insights on undiscovered treasures, local events, and tailored recommendations.

4. Virtual Tours and Apps:

Digital Exploration: Embark on virtual excursions of Lake Como with internet platforms and smartphone applications. Experience the majesty of the lake from the comfort of your home and arrange your on-site experiences using augmented reality tools.

5. Artistic Reverie:

Art Exhibitions: Seek for art exhibits presenting works inspired by Lake Como. Local galleries typically feature artwork expressing the visual poetry of the place.

6. Cooking Classes and Culinary Journeys:

Italian Culinary Exploration: Enroll in virtual cooking lessons or join culinary tours that explore the tastes of Lake Como. Elevate your palette with real recipes and culinary knowledge.

7. Social Media Inspirations:

Instagram, Pinterest, and More: Follow Lake Como-themed accounts on social media platforms for daily doses of inspiration. From magnificent sights to travel recommendations, social media is a dynamic canvas of discovery.

8. Travel Forums and Communities:

Interactive Discourse: Join travel forums and online communities where other lovers exchange experiences, tips, and travel tales. Engage in discussions to gather useful ideas and tips.

9. Podcasts and Audio Guides:

Auditory Exploration: Tune into podcasts that dig into Lake Como's history, culture, and travel tales. Audio tours may further improve your on-site experience with interesting commentary.

10. Event Calendars:

Local Events and Festivals: Stay current on Lake Como's event schedule. From cultural festivals to art exhibits, engaging in local activities improves your relationship with the place.

Traveler's Tips:

Bookmarking and Saving: Save online articles, guides, and resources for convenient reference throughout your travel.

Local applications: Download local applications for navigation, language translation, and real-time information about events and attractions.

Connect with Locals: Reach out to locals via social media or travel forums for customized suggestions and insights.

Your Enriching Odyssey Continues:

Lake Como's charm extends beyond its borders with these extra resources. As you accompany your tour with literary exploits, virtual discoveries, and gastronomic pleasures, may your relationship with this Italian gem develop, producing a tapestry of recollections that surpass the ordinary. Buon Viaggio!

Glossary of Local Terms

Embark on a linguistic voyage around Lake Como with this intriguing lexicon of local terminology, each word a lyrical note in the lovely song of Italian life. Immerse yourself in the linguistic tapestry of the area, allowing these words to become the lyrical threads weaving through your lakeside journey.

1. Aperitivo (A-pe-ri-ti-vo):

Culinary Prelude: An early evening tradition, it entails relishing a pre-dinner cocktail accompanied by delightful appetisers. Lakeside aperitivo offers a range of local tastes.

2. Passeggiata (Pas-se-gia-ta):

Evening Stroll: A leisurely evening stroll, frequently along the coastline or through lovely town squares. Join residents in the passeggiata to enjoy the lovely atmosphere.

3. Gelato (Je-la-to):

Artisanal Delight: Indulge in this Italian-style ice cream, available in a plethora of flavors. Gelato shops, like sweet serenades, entice you to relish a moment of gastronomic ecstasy.

4. Trattoria (Tra-tto-ria):

Local Eateries: Unlike formal restaurants, trattorias provide homey, traditional meals. Explore these quaint businesses for a true taste of Italian food.

5. Caffè (Caf-fe):

Coffee Culture: A vital component of Italian life, caffè comprises many coffee styles. Sip espresso at a lakeside café, appreciating the rich, fragrant coffee and the mood of lakeside reflections.

6. Vicolo (Vi-co-lo):

Cobbled Alleys: Wander through these small, cobblestone lanes that weave through cities, uncovering secret nooks and local treasures. Each vicolo speaks stories of history and charm.

7. Piazza (Piat-tsa):

Town Squares: Vibrant gathering spaces, frequently flanked by historic buildings and vibrant eateries. The piazza is the centre of any town, throbbing with the beat of local life.

8. Riva (Reeva):

Lakefront Promenade: Experience the lakeside charm by wandering along the river. Admire the picturesque vistas, architectural grandeur, and the soft lapping of waves on the coast.

9. Ciao (Chow):

Versatile Greeting: Embrace the pleasant attitude of Lake Como with "ciao," a multipurpose greeting meaning both "hello" and "goodbye." Connect with locals with this warm and friendly term.

10. Bella Vista (Bel-la Vis-ta):

Beautiful View: A word that wonderfully depicts the beautiful landscapes surrounding Lake Como. Whether atop a hill or at the water's edge, every turn gives a beautiful sight.

Your Linguistic Serenade:

As you explore the villages and appreciate the local culture, let this dictionary be your language guide—a lyrical companion harmonizing with the poetic beauty of Lake Como. Buon Viaggio!

Printed in Great Britain
by Amazon

45991219R00066